"EVERYWHERE WE GO PEOPLE NOTICE WHAT A FANTASTIC SWIM-
MER NORTH IS. THEY JUST CAN'T BELIEVE SOMEONE
SO YOUNG CAN SWIM SO WELL. WHILE WORKING WITH
MICHELLE, IT WAS A JOY TO SEE NORTH BECOME
EMPOWERED BY THE WATER."

- KIM KARDASHIAN WEST, TV PERSONALITY

"BOTH MY KIDS LEARNED TO SWIM THROUGH THIS
INNOVATIVE AND EFFECTIVE TEACHING METHOD.
IT MAKES THE PARENTS AND CHILDREN FEEL SAFE,
WHICH IS THE MOST IMPORTANT PART."

- SARAH MICHELLE GELLAR, ACTRESS

"OUR CHILDREN HAVE VERY DIFFERENT PERSONALITIES.
MICHELLE'S SPIRITUAL, MODERN APPROACH WORKED
BEAUTIFULLY AND TURNED BOTH OF OUR KIDS INTO
STRONG, CONFIDENT SWIMMERS."

**- ROBBIE WILLIAMS, SINGER-SONGWRITER
AYDA WILLIAMS, ACTRESS**

"THREE OF MY CHILDREN STARTED LESSONS WHEN THEY WERE
TWO YEARS OLD. THEY WERE POOL SAFE BY TWO AND A HALF.
KNOWING IF MY CHILDREN EVER FELL INTO A POOL THEY COULD
EASILY SWIM TO SAFETY IS LIFE CHANGING."

– AMANDA BROWN, AUTHOR OF *LEGALLY BLONDE*

Michelle is a world-class swim instructor and travels around the globe to work with a wide variety of high-profile clients. She has taught thousands of lessons and created countless safe, joyful swimmers. This is her method.

Such a joy Swimming with your Little one!

Yo-r Michelle

A Mermaid's Guide

Empower Your Child in Water and in Life

Written by:
Michelle Lang

Swim teaching techniques developed by:
Michelle Lang and Ian Nelms

www.RelaxationBasedLifestyle.com

Discover upcoming books from Michelle Lang

Where the Sanity Ends:
A humorous parody of "Where the Sidewalk Ends" for parents with toddlers.

Children's books coming soon:

Bernie the Bubble

Toddy the Dot

Under the Rug

With gratitude to my Mom for being my first swim teacher in London and for spending countless hours editing this book. To my dad, sisters, T, EV, and COCO. You make my heart full.

Thank you.

SWIM IN WATER & GIVE WATER

10% OF AUTHOR ROYALTIES ARE DONATED TO WATER RELATED NOT-FOR-PROFITS, INCLUDING WWW.WATERTOTHRIVE.ORG.

A Mermaid's Guide by Michelle Lang
Swim teaching techniques developed by Michelle Lang & Ian Nelms

© 2018 RBL STUDIOS
Published in 2019

For permissions contact:
Assist@relaxationbasedlifestyle.com

Edited by: Deborah M. Lang
Special Thanks: Jessica Allen, Heather Fowler
and Ngoc Nguyen
Water photography by: Ian Nelms
Headshot photography by: Bob Turton
Cover design by: Leslie K

ISBN: 978-1-7322636-0-4
Ebook ISBN: 978-1-7322636-1-1

www.SwimYogi.Com
www.RelaxationBasedLifestyle.Com

First Edition

-Table of Contents-

INTRODUCTION

Drowning is the number one cause of accidental death for children ages 1-4, even over car accidents[1]. But what if I told you there's a way to create strong, joyful swimmers without the anxiety typically associated with taking swim lessons? What if you could discover simple tips and phrases to use with your child to avoid inadvertently giving your child bad water habits? What if learning to swim can, and should be, one of the most empowering experiences of your child's life?

All of this is possible and this book will be your guide. The good news is, learning to swim is NOT complicated. It can be broken down into three simple phases:

1) Going under the water
2) Moving through the water
3) Popping up for breaths

Even if you don't want to teach your child to swim yourself, by reading this book, you'll gain knowledge and an overwhelming sense of peace by simply learning how the water works and why infusing your child's journey with Relaxation Based Swimming is so important.

Relaxation Based Swimming is a modern, highly effective and proven method created by Michelle Lang and Ian Nelms, who have brought thousands of children through successful swim journeys over the past, combined, twenty-five years of teaching.

Inside these pages, you will find over 50 photos, progression and personality charts, illustrations, and case studies to guide you. A Mermaid's Guide not only instructs you how to create a safe, joyful swimmer, it also shares 5 simple communication tips to use with your child. These "Mermaid Golden Rules" will arm you with the tools you need to help your child gracefully overcome challenges both in and out of the pool.

After reading, you'll be able to identify if the swimming lessons you're taking your child to are productive or ineffective. You'll also learn the ONE primary bathtub skill to teach you child that will save you hundreds of dollars on swimming lessons!

Through your patience and perseverance, you can become the peaceful parent lounging by the side of the pool watching your child swim with a latte in hand. (Instead of being riddled with anxiety every time your child is around water.) As Amanda Brown, author of Legally Blonde says, "Three of my children started lessons when they were two years old. They were pool safe by two and a half. Knowing if my children ever fell into a pool they could easily swim to safety is life changing."

Give your child the gift of becoming a strong, confident swimmer. *It's a skill they will take with them their entire life.*

So turn the page, and dive in!

*Relaxation Based Swimming is a subsidiary of RBL (pronounced "rebel") STUDIOS. RBL stands for **R**elaxation **B**ased **L**ifestyle and is a multi-faceted company founded by Michelle Lang and Ian Nelms. Visit www.RelaxationBasedLifestyle.com and **subscribe** to get the short, insightful, and myth busting blog series, **"27 Mermaid Secrets About Swimming, Revealed"** delivered into your inbox. Five minutes to read. Insights for life. Starting May 1st, 2019.*

CHAPTER ONE:
MINDSET OF RELAXATION BASED SWIMMING

What's your swim story? Did your Aunt Hildy toss you into the deep end thinking you will figure it out? Were you lined up on the edge of a cold pool with twelve other squirming children? Did your dad tell you to swim to him to get the new toy car you wanted? More importantly, what is your relationship with the water now?

The first step to Relaxation Based Swimming is an understanding that learning to swim should be a fantastic experience. You get to fly in the water!

When we frame swimming as an exciting opportunity, the process can be seamless. Sure, there will be hurdles to overcome within the overall experience, but the discovery, as a whole, should be empowering. Your children will delight in the knowledge that they can overcome obstacles if they keep trying. Every lesson will have tangible evidence of their tenacity paying off. What an excellent microcosm for life!

What if your child dislikes the water, in spite of the positivity you've built surrounding it? What if they refuse to put their face under or even put their toe in on the top step? For these children, their journey may start out with a more colorful beginning. Once they understand the water, take ownership of it, and pass through their fear, their love for swimming will shine even brighter. In over 25 years of teaching swimming, my husband and myself have never encountered a child who can't learn to swim. Some don't like it initially, but all love it by the end.

Having emotional empathy is a vital part of the process. (Not sympathy, empathy. You shouldn't feel bad for your child. They are learning an exciting new life skill.) But you should, however, simply acknowledge their emotional state. (More on how to do this effectively later.)

Children are incredibly perceptive and can read even the smallest micro-emotions[2]. If you are genuinely excited for them, they will feel it. Their openness to learn stems from your deep belief they are capable (more on this in Chapter two: Being the Buddha). Your little one must be guided through the physical, emotional, and spiritual part of learning to swim in a mindful way. This attitude will ensure that their love for the water will be carried with them for a lifetime.

COUNTER INTUITIVE PROBLEM:

Swimming is a counter-intuitive problem. If you fall into the water and you don't know how to swim, your natural instinct is to thrash and scream. If you thrash and scream, you exasperate the problem by eliminating the oxygen in your system and making your muscles contract, which makes you sink! If you know how to use the water's natural buoyancy and if you stay calm, you can easily swim to safety.

Counter-intuitive problems take practice to train your system how to react when the situation arises[3]. It's like skidding on a patch of ice. Your body wants to turn the steering wheel away, but you actually need to turn into the spin. The only way to learn this, and make it a part of your core memory, is to practice. You have to keep practicing how to react, so if the situation arises, panic doesn't override your logic. It must be woven into your muscle memory. Swimming is the same.

SWIMMING:

Swimming is moving from point A to point B in an intentional way and without external forces such as undercurrent or momentum. Strokes are easy to implement once core relaxation and body control are established. If children learn to do strokes, but never learn how to float and relax in the water, they will never be an excellent swimmer.

POOL SAFE vs. SWIM SAFE*:

Pool Safe is the first layer of becoming Swim Safe. When your child can jump in, turn and swim back to the wall, your child is Pool Safe. They must be able to swim with intention, hold their breath correctly, and have the mental wherewithal to get themselves to safety.

Swim Safe is what you must strive for. Having a Swim Safe swimmer is being able to sit by the side of the pool watching your child swim without teetering on the edge of your cabana chair thinking you are going to have to jump in after them at any second. A Swim Safe swimmer is confident, can pop up for breaths, knows their limitations and can think clearly in difficult situations. If they catch a mouthful of water, they can recover. If they get tired, they can still make it to the edge. If they find themselves under an intertube, they have the mental toughness and grit to get themselves out. **No human is ever drown proof, and everyone should be under supervision when swimming**, but you want your child as Swim Safe as possible.

We teach swimming in three phases. Each phase has its own chapter and this book will go into much more detail in the remaining pages, but here is a brief overview:

*No child is ever 100% water safe. You MUST watch your swimmer at ALL times.

THE BASICS:

Phase 1) Going underwater/floating

This phase includes swimmers learning to hold their breath correctly, glides, and floats. Floating is crucial to being a truly relaxed swimmer. Do not skip this phase unless you have a child under two and a half who isn't physically capable of isolating and controlling different parts of their body (in this case, floats and glides are taught along with phase two, and then floats are introduced once the child is a little older). But always focus on proper breath control, even if layering in swimming at the same time.

Phase 2) Moving through the water (kicking/propelling)

Phase 2 has two parts: swimming and swimming with intention. Swimming is moving from point A to point B without assistance. If the swimmer can be released into the water and move independently, they are swimming. Swimming with intention is being able to propel forward, sideways, turn, and get from point to point. Swimmers who can swim with intention have an awareness of how much breath they have left in relation to the distance they must swim to get to safety. Swimming with intention is crucial for pool and swim safety.

Phase 3) Popping up for breaths

Phase three is teaching how to pop up for breaths.

This book will focus on these three phases. If your little one is confident floating, using their energy correctly, and allowing the water to hold them up, strokes will be easy to add on later.

After phase three is accomplished, there's a bonus phase called The Push Through. This phase focuses on mental toughness and has preparatory exercises to train your swimmer's minds to overcome panic and problem solve.

Before we get in the pool, you must have a foundation of communication and trust with your little one. This leads us to the next chapter: THE MERMAID GOLDEN RULES.

CHAPTER TWO:
5 MERMAID GOLDEN RULES

The Mermaid Golden Rules have been developed over thousands of lessons during the past, combined, 25 years of teaching. You can use these techniques both in and out of the water. They are highly effective and are the foundation for creating a peaceful, trusting, and respectful relationship with your children.

1. AHM: Acknowledge, Hug and Move On

AHM (Acknowledge, Hug and Move On) is the foundation of RBL (Relaxation Based Lifestyle) philosophy. Although AHM was developed in the water, AHM works in and out of the pool. It can be life altering for you and your child. I use this countless times in my day, both with my own kids and the children I teach.

Think of clearing your throat: Ahhhmmm.

A: Acknowledge the feeling

H: Hug the emotion

M: Move on

Children don't understand that the things we deem "not important" are actually not important. To them, they are! So although your request to put the toy dinosaur back, or put their swim suit on, may seem inconsequential to you...to them, it's the worst thing of their lives! A quick and easy "solve" is to simply AHM.

Acknowledge:

Try saying, "I see you don't want to put on your swim suit." or "I see you want that dinosaur." If your child is worked up, you may have to say this a few times so they hear you. Give them a moment to understand that *you* understand. They don't have to stop crying or asking for what they want, but make sure you have their attention before moving onto the next part.

Hug their emotions:

Say, "I see you don't want to wear your swimsuit. I'm telling you to put it on, and you don't want to. That is frustrating." or "I see you want the dinosaur. I'm telling you to put it away, and that makes you angry. It's okay to feel upset sometimes." Chances are they will stop resisting at this point. You finally get what they are saying!

Move on:

Then move on and say, "I know you don't want to, but we have to put the suit on. I see you don't want to wear it, so after the lesson we can take it off again." or "I know you don't want to, but you have to put the toy back. It's okay to be upset, but you have to take deep breaths. I'll help you."

Most of the time, if children feel like you understand them, they will go with the flow. Everyone wants to feel understood[4]. Kids aren't any different. The only difference is kids often don't have the language or the eloquence to express their needs, wants or desires in a way that will help them feel understood. They express their needs simply, in one way, over and over again. If you simply Acknowledge their want, Hug their emotion and Move On, your child will feel understood and more at peace.

One more thing about the "Move On" part. There will be times in the pool, and in life, when your child has to come up against adversity. The challenge could be simply catching a tiny mouthful of water or merely putting their eyes under the water for the first time. If it's the first time this situation happens, your little one will have no idea how to react. They have never experienced it before! In the pool, say your little ones go under for the first time and they throw their hands to their face and cry. They didn't drink the water, but it's a new experience and they are shocked and a little scared. Instead of rushing to get a towel and coddling them, try saying, "You went under water, it feels funny to be under the water" (Acknowledge). Once they look at you like they understand that you understand, go to the next step. "It does feel funny" (Hug) and then say, "You did great. You went under the water. Let's go back to the pool's steps!" (Move On).

You've acknowledged the fact they experienced something new and hard. You've labeled it, and you didn't give it a ton of time because it's something they need to get used to. If you spend 10 minutes re-living the experience, they are going to think it's worth 10 minutes of sympathy. It shouldn't be given even one second of sympathy. It's exciting, they put their eyes under water! You should give it five to ten seconds of empathy as you use AHM.

Pretend your little one is gliding out to you and they catch a tiny mouthful of water. They come up coughing. You say, "Ewww. You drank the water! That's yucky." You can do some coughs to show them you understand. I like to throw some humor in and say, "Did it taste like a burrito?" to make them laugh. And then I hug the emotion "It did taste yucky." and move on. "Take a good breath before you go under, because you don't want to drink the water!"

Let's say your little one was trying to get a toy and mistimed their breath and got a batch of water up their nose. You can tell it hurt. Your little one comes up and immediately begins to howl. Say, "Oooo, that hurt! Water up your nose! Yuck! That hurts! That hurts!" Once you have their attention, move onto the next step. "Sometimes you get water up your nose. It doesn't feel good" (Hug). "If you get water up your nose you can HUMMMM. That's your secret power against water up your nose. Try it! HUMMMMMM" (Move On).

Obviously, the bigger the emotional or physical pain, the longer the hug part can be. But try not to make the Hug longer than what the children will, eventually, learn to dedicate to the event. You don't want to dismiss their feelings, even with a small injury, but you do want them to learn the way you would like them, eventually, to handle it themselves.

MERMAID TIP: Skinned knees

My two-year-old son was very sensitive to anything having to do with blood. If he skinned his knee, I would coddle and hold him until he calmed down, even if it was the tiniest of wounds. His recovery would sometimes take hours! My son must have thought he was horrifically injured because I was giving him so much attention. I was re-enforcing his idea about his wound being traumatic. It got so intense that I would dread going outside for fear he would fall and the rest of the day would be ruined. I wanted to be sensitive to his pain, but I realized I had taught him to give each skinned knee an extremely long shelf life. Once I gave the wound as much time as I thought he should, we had a much better time exploring the world. I encourage you to be empathetic but don't give a paper cut the same amount of emotional energy, as you would, say, a bloody knee. Your child, initially, doesn't know the difference. To them, the paper cut may feel like the worst thing in the world (up to that point in their life, it may be!). It's your job to guide them about how much time and energy should be spent on each discomfort encountered. But always acknowledge their emotion, give it a hug, and then move on.

2. BE THE BUDDHA

Children are bundles of raw emotion. Joy, frustration, sadness, and fear all flow freely from them. The emotional variance can be overwhelming, but it doesn't have to be. Your job is not to "fix" your child's emotions. (More on this later!) You aren't in control of what *they* are feeling. But you are in control of what *you* are feeling. If you're calm, relaxed, and unwavering, you open the door to success for both you and your child.

Reiki:

Reiki is a healing technique based on the principle that the therapist can channel energy into the patient's body through touch[5]. Reiki talks a lot about chi, or body energy. By controlling your body's energy, you will influence the energy of others. If your inner energy is fast and uncertain, your child's energy will match it. As a certified Reiki practitioner, I can assure you, it works. Especially on children[6].

You can use your calming energy both in and out of the water. Of course, "Being the Buddha" is harder to maintain for an extended period of time. Who can be the Buddha every second of their life? Maybe monks? But I bet even they have frustrations from time to time. Ultimately, Relaxation Based Swimming (and lifestyle) isn't about being calm every moment of your day. It's about accepting whatever emotional state you are in, hugging your feelings, and moving on.

In the water, however, you should strive to be the beacon of serenity. For a set amount of time, you can "Be the Buddha."

BUDDHA REPELLENT:

Nerves, cold water, and anxiety can all inhibit your Buddha-like state. Try to eliminate anything negatively influencing your body energy. One of the most significant culprits hindering Buddha-like behavior is frustration. Frustration is the gap between expectations and reality. Try to eliminate as many sources of potential frustration as you can.

Tips to becoming the Buddha.

1) Have a singular focus. Try to focus on only one child. If you have two children and one is crying by the edge of the pool as you try to teach the other child, frustration begins. Have a care-taker or friend watch your other child so you can focus on the one in the pool.

2) Eliminate expectations. To eliminate your expectations, place all of your energy into the child and soak up what is actually happening in front of you. You may want them to stop crying, have fun, and to focus, but if that's not what's happening at the moment, it's okay. Be at peace with your child's current state, no matter what it is. Once you are at peace with the current situation, then you can navigate your

child out of their emotional turmoil and into your sea of calmness if need be.

3) Be honest with yourself. Are you still nervous? Where do the nerves come from? If you're not ready to have your little one in the water, it will be that much harder for them to learn. Trust in them and their ability to achieve. You can also try accepting your nerves. It's okay to be a little nervous. But if you find yourself riddled with tension and anxiety, it would be best to have a professional swim instructor guide you through the process. Or, perhaps you will feel you're more ready after reading the remainder of the book. Sometimes nerves come from "the unknown." Once you understand how the process works, you may find yourself empowered and ready to teach.

4) Warm up the pool! Learning to swim in cold water is tough. When you are chilly, your muscles are constricted and it's not only hard to float, but it's also hard to focus. If you can, try to find a pool or have a pool heated to about 90 degrees Fahrenheit. In the article by Jeff Herman at Livestrong.com he states, "Cold water zaps your body heat 25 times quicker than cold air." The warmer the pool, the more relaxed you and your little ones will be and the easier it will be to teach. (Note: don't teach in a pool or hot tub over 95 degrees. It's not healthy for your child to be too hot[7].)

MERMAID TIP: Breaths

Take deep breaths. Your breaths control your conscious[8]. Accept any feelings that come to your mind. Breathe low and slow. Tell yourself that your child can learn to be comfortable in the pool. Eliminate expectations. It's okay if your little one cries, it's okay if they have a tough time, and okay if they love it. Be open to everything and you won't be disappointed. Go into every lesson with a game plan, but remember to be the Buddha.

It's the one thing you can always control.

3. THE PROMISE

What if your husband told you he was going to take out the trash, but he never did? What if your wife promised you she would be at your dinner party, but continually stood you up? You wouldn't have a very trusting relationship, would you? What if your spouse said they would pass you the peas, and they didn't? Even something so small would probably make you feel frustrated. Why didn't they pass the peas when they said they were going to?

THE PROMISE:

Be clear with your child, and always follow through. This is how trust is built[9]. No one can relax unless they trust the person and the situation. This is true both in and out of the water, but in the water, there is so much uncertainty that the truism is magnified. The more your child feels like they can count on you, the more at peace they will be.

You may say, "It's hard to always to follow through!" It's not. All you have to do is take extra time to think about what you are going to do, say, or ask. You are the one setting the standard. You are the one making the promise, and you are in control of following through, so take the extra time. It's okay to sit in silence a few moments as you ponder. Chances are your little one won't even notice! Children are much more comfortable with silence than adults are and it's good for children to have "solo" play[10]. They are involved with what they are doing. So, while you ponder the next activity or request, they most likely will find a way to entertain themselves by splashing or reaching for a toy. These empty space activities are brilliant.

> **MERMAID TIP: Empty space**
> Children discover a lot in the absence of instruction[11]. Try to allow them empty space moments even if you aren't thinking about your next request.

If your child happens to ask what you're doing as you sit in silence…just tell them you're thinking.

Once you decide the next activity or task, let them know what it is and then follow through. Never ask them to do something they can't do. If they haven't learned how to hold their breath properly, you don't want to ask them to glide out to you. Make sure you ask them to do an achievable activity (you wouldn't ask a gymnast to do a back flip if they can't do a cartwheel yet. In the same way, swimming is best learned in tiny, achievable steps). If you ask your child to do something they can't do, the trust will be broken. But if you ask them to do something they can do, but they just don't want to do (or they think is too hard) once they try and succeed, their confidence and courage will grow.

The Promise isn't about bossing your child around. It's about being clear with your words and instructions. It's about thinking before you speak and making sure you always follow through. It's about being a leader! A good leader harnesses the goals of their followers and guides them to success in a calm, yet firm way.

MERMAID TIP: HELP! I didn't follow through!
Let's pretend you tell your child they are going under water on three, and you count 1,2, and by three you hesitate and you don't follow through. Don't stress out about it. Obviously, we want to guard against this as much as possible, but it happens and you'll only make the situation worse if you let it rattle you. Simply re-connect with your child. Be the Buddha. Clear the pallet with a different activity and re-set to try again later. The next time be sure to follow through! You don't want to create a habit by not following through two or three times in a row. It's better to ask the child to do less, and follow through on what you do ask than to ask the child to do a lot of things, but only follow through some of the time.

4. HAND TO HEART (H2H), EMPOWERMENT PHRASES (EP), and MIRROR AND AGREE (M&A)

Hand 2 Heart (H2H):

In Reiki, the heart is the fourth of the seven main Chakras[12]. The heart Chakra is the emotional center for inner peace, joy and love. Place your hand on your child's heart. Give your child a gentle squeeze. Channel positive energy. Hold your little one securely, look them in the eye with your shoulders squarely to them and say, "I'm here to keep you safe. I promise. I'll always tell you what we are going to do." (Or whatever phrase is appropriate at the time.)

Empowerment Phrases (EP):

In addition to the physical H2H, use empowerment phrases such as:

a.   "You can do this."

b.   "I'm right here, I'll keep you safe."

c.   "The water holds you up. Isn't it amazing?"

d.   "Did you know you can fly in the water?"

e.   "You're in control of the water."

f.   "You're the boss of the water. You tell it what to do."

There's something to be said about positive affirmations and empowerment phrases. As Vanessa Van Hess, an expert on behavior, says in her book, Captivate, "Great expectations are met with greatness." And studies performed by Robert Rosenthal and Lenore Jacobson show teacher's expectations of their students impact how successful the student becomes[13].

I use many empowerment phrases during lessons, particularly at the beginning of class to set the intention and soothe the child. I use hand to heart in conjunction with empowerment phrases to ramp up the effect.

Mirror and Agree (M&A):

Imagine telling your spouse you want to take a three-week vacation to Italy:

YOU: I want to go to Italy! Wouldn't that be fun?
HUBBY: No, we're not doing that. It's expensive and we don't have the money.

How would you feel? Most likely you would feel bad about expressing your thoughts in the first place. But how would you feel if the conversation went like this?

YOU: I want to go to Italy! Wouldn't that be fun?
HUBBY: Yeah! That would be amazing. I can taste the gelato now. I wish we had the money, but maybe we can start a savings account and put a little towards the trip when we can!

HUBBY: I know you've always wanted to go to Italy! It would be amazing. We don't have enough money saved to go to Italy, but how about a fancy trip to San Diego instead?

The outcome of all three conversations are the same: you're not going to Italy, but the feelings behind the conversations are incredibly different.

Mirror and Agree (M&A) is an extension of AHM. Let's take a closer look!

Example:
CHILD: I want OUT! I WANT OUT!!!
YOU: (Mirror their distress at about 50% to show you understand.) You want out, you want out. Okay, okay! Let me help you! I'll help you get out. We just need to ask each toy what they want to see, and then you can get out!

You can also MIRROR and AGREE.

CHILD: I want to get OUT! OUT!
YOU: You want to get out! You don't want to go swimming. I want to get out too. I'll help you! Let's do five glides, play the dolphin game and then we can get out!

Mirror and Agree is a great tool for every day life with children (and everyone else too, for that matter!).

> **MERMAID TIP: Movement mirrors**
> You can also mirror your child's movements to form a bond (this works particularly well with children two and under). If the child splashes the water in front of them with their hand, you can splash water in front of you with your hand. If they blow bubbles, you blow bubbles! Mirroring shows a connection and tells them "you are alike." People like people who are like them[14]. It's human nature. So use the same body language your swimmer is using to create a shared experience.

"You don't have to always agree, but you have to disagree nicely."

– Me, several times a day.

In life you will not always get your way. It's okay to disagree, but I always say, "You have to disagree nicely."

With children, you may spend a lot of your time disagreeing with what they want to do. If something is dangerous, obviously, you don't have to agree with their desire to do it…but you can still share their sentiment so you aren't making them feel bad for their expressed idea.

For example:

TWO YEAR OLD: I…jump…that.
YOU: You want to dive off of the thirty foot high dive! That does look like fun. It's a long way down, and I'm not going to let you do that because it's my job to keep you safe.

It's always okay to disagree, but we need to disagree nicely.

5. BLANKETING

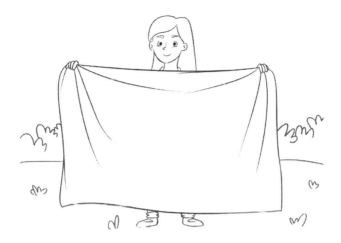

Let's pretend you are learning to do a fire burn (you've decided to be a stunt person! Congrats!). You get in the special clothing, and you look at Bill, the instructor. Bill avoids your eyes and his shoulders are slumped. His gaze darts side to side and he mumbles something about you being just fine as he lights you on fire. You wouldn't have much confidence, would you?

There are several parts to blanketing: body, voice and spirit.

1) BODY

There are many things you can do physically to communicate effectively with your children. First, stand squarely in front of them with your eyes an inch or so above theirs. Not so much that you are overpowering, but in a way that says, I'm in charge, you can trust me. If you are both standing, this won't work. You have to lower to their level. When you use blanketing to communicate a new idea or activity, keep your shoulders back and square to the child. Be sure to be the Buddha and keep your gaze locked on theirs. If they look away, it's okay. But you are the one to hold their gaze as long as they will hold it.

> **MERMAID TIP: Eye contact**
>
> Have a little one who isn't big into eye contact? Want to get their attention? Just say, "Where are my eyes?" Most likely that will get them to look right at you.
>
> Have a child who loves eye contact? Children will hold your gaze much longer than adults. Use it! Holding your child's gaze can be a connecting experience[15].

2) Voice: Language and tone

As grownups, we often speak in code. We say things like:

ADULT: Would you like to go to the meeting soon?
(What you are really saying is)
ADULT: We have to go to the meeting right now because we are going to be late! Hurry up!

Between two adults, the following type of conversation would be rare, but with children, it's typical!

ADULT 1: Can you please hand me the sprinkles?
ADULT 2: I can't. I'm eating my ice cream.

Young children don't have many cultural formalities in play yet. So if you're asking them a question, and they don't do whatever it is you're asking, chances are they won't!

During lessons, if you want your child to listen, you must phrase your requests in a way that gives them the best chance of success. Instead of saying, "Could you put the toy on the wall?" try saying, "I want you to put the toy on the wall." By re-phasing with a clear, direct message you're much more likely to have the results you desire.

BUT ISN'T IT RUDE TO ASK LIKE THAT?

No. I think politeness to kids is great. I use it all the time to model kind and acceptable behavior. "Please pick the toy up from the first step" is lovely. I say it often. That said, it may not be the most effective way to communicate when working with a new and difficult task[16].

Instead, I use H2H, blanketing and say, "I want you to pick up the toy from the first step." I never ask a child a question if it's not really a question. Asking questions maybe the polite "adult" behavior, but it's not fair to children who should be able to exercise their right to say, "No!"

MERMAID TIP: Who's the leader?

There's a wave of parenting which encourages parents to ask kids for permission for everything. I like the idea of giving our children respect by asking for their permission, but your toddler's brain isn't developed enough to make certain life decisions. They shouldn't have to be learning how to grow up and also be responsible for every decision along the way. It's too much.

Imagine starting a huge new job you've never done before. How would you feel if your boss always asked your permission to do everything? What if your boss let you make all the decisions? Wouldn't it make you feel anxious to feel like YOU were in charge of your leader? But if your boss listened to your opinions and guided your ideas to achieve success, even if you didn't agree with her all the time, chances are you would feel safe and empowered.

Children thrive with structure and kind leadership[17]. Often, asking too many questions is going to give them anxiety. Especially when it comes to the water. Plus, if you ask a child if they want to put their face under the water, and they say no, you shouldn't disrespect their words and put them under the water anyway. (Remember THE PROMISE!) What is really rude is asking for their permission and not respecting their reply.

That said, if you are genuinely asking if they want to go underwater, that's okay. The top priority of Relaxation Based Swimming is to make everyone feel at ease. There are no right answers other than the one you ground yourself in. So if you want to ask your child if they want to go underwater, and you're okay with not putting them under unless they consent, then that's okay. But it's important to be aware of the situation and understand how you could communicate if you wanted to guide your little one through their fears. (Because, after all, a child cannot learn to swim if they can't go underwater.)

The concept is the same with potty training or anything else. If it's not a choice, don't ask them. Try saying, "It's time to go potty" vs "Would you like to go potty?" or you can ask a question, "Would you like to use the big potty, or the little potty?" Because if you ask a yes or no question, and they say no…it's not fair to ignore their answer. It's great to let your little one in on the action and give choices. Just make sure, when you do, you are okay with whatever they pick!

TONE OF VOICE: Pace, Pitch, and Volume.

How you say things is just as important as what you say. There are a few parts to Tone: Pace, Pitch and Volume.

For your pacing, it's important to speak slower than usual. Kids are incredibly smart, but if you talk too quickly, they may not catch what you're saying. Think about when you go to a new country, and you are learning the language. If a local starts to talk to you at one hundred words a minute, the chances of you grasping what they are saying are small. But if they slow down their speech, just enough to let you catch up, then you'd probably understand most of the conversation.

When thinking about the Pitch of your voice, keep in mind high voices often get categorized as "unimportant." Kids hear high, fast, voices all day long. It is easy for them to zone them out. It's amazing how much a lower pitch can impact the outcome.

You can also change the volume of your voice. I find whispering to be one of the most effective tools of teaching. When you whisper, the child has to lean in and really listen to what you're saying. It's also fun because it makes it sound like whatever you're saying is a secret!

3) Spirit

Spirit might be a section to take up with your psychologist, but let's touch on it anyway!

Parenting is hard; you're often trying to do five things at once. It's easy to feel split between your needs and your children's needs. Often, both aren't met in the fullest way possible.

Teaching your little one to swim is a chance to take refuge. You cannot, or should not, be doing anything else when you are teaching. During the 10 (or more) minutes in the pool, you must be a clear channel. Teaching someone to swim can be a form of meditation. You get to be the light, the peace, the island of calm. If you're frazzled, nervous, or upset, you'll have a less effective lesson.

Lessons are a chance to connect with your child. Allow whatever is going on in front of you to soak into you. If your child is crying, accept their tears. Wrap your child in the protective shield of your serenity and eliminate expectations. Blanket them! Be big, warm, and soothing, but also strong and expansive. Your child must understand you are there to keep them safe. They have to feel like you truly understand them and empathize with them. Open yourself up and invite them in.

CHAPTER 3:
5 KEY BATHTUB EXERCISES

Is your child too young for lessons? Or you don't have a pool but you want to give your child a head start? Perfect. There are quite a few activities you can do to help your child be ready for swimming lessons even before they get in a pool. If you can teach them ONE skill (how to hold their breath under the water) in the tub, you could save hundreds of dollars on swimming lessons.

1) POURING WATER OVER THEIR HEADS

GOAL: From an early age pour (or trickle) water over your child's head as you wash their hair. The earlier you introduce the feeling of water coming over their face the more used to it they will become.

AGE: 3 months plus

HOW: Say, "Little Love, water is going to come over your head on the count of three." Give them a 1,2,3 count and then pour (or trickle) water over their head and faces. If you start the routine early enough, they will not mind it. Pour (or trickle) water over their head about three to five times every time they have a bath. Eventually, they will learn how to hold their breath. Start with small amounts of water, say a half cup. As they get older and have better breath control, you pour half a cup. And then you can do a full cup etc...

> **MERMAID TIP: Coughing**
> Usually, coughing is a natural expulsion of water. Be sure to read
> Chapter 13 for more information. Knowing how to hold their breath
> could save your child's life. Start teaching them early! (Ask your
> pediatrician if you have questions about the safety or if your little one
> has any extenuating circumstances or illnesses.)

As you pour water over your little one's head, be sure to focus on your micro-expressions. Keep your face calm and serene. Your little one will be looking at you to see how they should respond[18]. If you're cringing as you dribble the water over their face, then they will be scared. Be clear and always follow through. 1,2,3-pour. Be sure to use empowerment phrases and AHM (Acknowledge, Hug and Move on).

MY CHILD DOESN'T LIKE WATER ON THEIR FACE! WHAT SHOULD I DO?

An initial discomfort to having water on their face is common. For a child over six months old, try taking three bath toys and placing them on the side of the tub. Tell your little one you'll be doing one pour over their head for each toy. Having a visual end point and set number can help them, and you, relax. If you can teach your child how to handle the feeling of water pouring over their face and how to hold their breath, they will have an advantage when they take swimming lessons.

2) BREATH UP, BUBBLES DOWN AND BREATH UP, Pufferfish

GOAL: Breath control

AGE: Twelve months and up (or whenever your little one has head/neck control)

HOW: Demonstrate taking a breath up above the water and then blowing bubbles into the tub. Repeat. Babies might not do it right away, but they will be watching you closely. Keep repeating the bubble blowing and, eventually, they will join in. NOTE: This is NOT to teach them how to blow bubbles under the water every time they submerge. This is to give them a visualization of their breath works.

For Breath Up, Pufferfish have them take a breath up, and then hold their breath under the water. To demonstrate, take a big breath and puff your cheeks out like a pufferfish. You can add onto this exercise by having your child open their eyes underwater and explore. By practicing holding their breath in the bathtub they are beginning the first, and often hardest, phase of swimming.

3) Bathtub Back Float

GOAL: Relaxation and trust

AGE: Six months and up

HOW: Lay your child on their back, holding their head in your hands. Look into their eyes, sing a song or smile and talk to them.

4) Kickies and STILL

AGE: Twelve months and up (or whenever your little one has head/neck control)

HOW: Have the water low enough so your child can put their arms on the bottom of the tub and keep their face out of the water. Then have them use their kicks to "Splash! Splash! Splash!"

Then say, "Still!" Have them keep their legs straight behind them. Being able to isolate and understand the difference between kickies and being still will help them in their swim journey.

5) RECOVERY

GOAL: Safety

AGE: Usually twelve to eighteen months, or when your child is physically capable.

HOW: If your child tips over in the bath, guide them the first few times to show them how to flip onto their bellies, get their hands under them and push themselves up.

Once you feel they understand how to get themselves back up (and are physically capable of doing so) it's okay to let them try themselves.

Drowning can happen in only two inches of water[19]. It's better for little ones to learn how to recover from tipping over when you are there to make sure they are safe versus if they tip over and someone is distracted and doesn't see them. Teach your child to recover so they are physically capable of doing so on their own. (Of course, safety comes first. Make sure they understand how to recover before they try on their own and help them if needed.)

For a video of these exercises visit: www.AMermaidsGuide.com or email me at assist@relaxationbasedlifestyle.com with the email subject: BATHTUB EXERCISES.

CHAPTER 4:
FAQ, Lesson Prep, Floaties, Sunscreen, and Other Tips.

WHEN IS THE BEST TIME TO START SWIM LESSONS?

You can start lessons as early as three months (or when your pediatrician says it is safe for your child). When you start lessons all depends on your time and resources. Let's say it takes six lessons for a two-year-old to properly accomplish phase 1 (submerge/float and glide). For a three-year-old, phase one could take about three lessons. An eighteen month old, however, could take eight to ten lessons to accomplish phase one.

The fastest rate of progression will be when the child is between 2 to 4 years old. Thusly, I recommend starting children between 2 and 3. That said, babies, as young as nineteen months old, are capable of swimming across the pool with breaths if given enough time and instruction. Just be sure to start your swimmer sometime before they are five-years-old. (At five-years-old your child's brain acts more like an adult's brain[20]. They have already formed their ideas about the pool, water, and swimming.)

CAN MY 18- 23 MONTH OLD TAKE LESSONS?

Yes, a child under two can swim. Email us at Connect@ relaxationbasedlifestyle with the title: PROGRESSION OF A SWIMMER and we will send you a video of the capabilities of children swimming at various ages! No child is drown-proof, but if your child can jump in, swim to the side, and get out, this could save their life. At 22-24 months old, most children have the strength and coordination to pop up for breaths, if given the time and energy it takes to teach them.

HOW LONG WILL IT TAKE FOR MY LITTLE ONE TO LEARN TO SWIM?

Every child is different. Swimming is a lot like walking. (The "normal" time babies learn to walk is 9-17 months[21].) Every child is different. Their rate of swim progression will depend on their personality, age, and physical development (chapter 11). On average, however, most children progress as follows.

AGES 18 months – Two Years

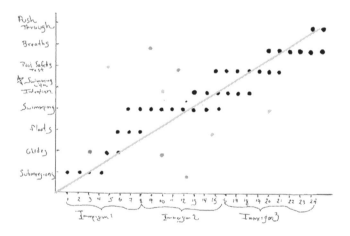

CHART: The number of lessons is horizontal, and the phase landmarks are vertical. Every now and then a student falls outside the "normal" progression chart. Every child is different and their swim progression will be as unique as they are!

AGES Two and a half to Three

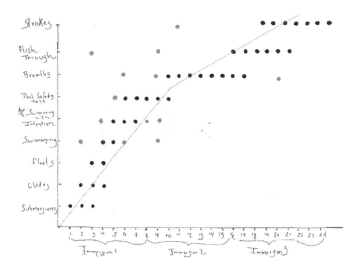

AGES Three and a Half to Four and a Half

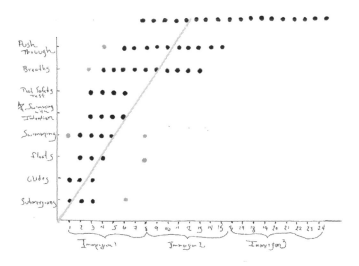

The progression charts on the previous page are charting progression when you take lessons from myself or someone else trained by my team. For lessons you do with your little one following this method, double the number of lessons it will take per phase. The reason you double the number of lessons is because you are learning how to teach the method at the same time your little one is learning to swim.

I'M TAKING MY CHILD TO SWIM LESSONS, WHAT DO I DO IF THEY CRY?

The best thing to do is acknowledge the emotion, hug it and then move onto the positive things they did during the lesson. The temptation is to put emphasis on the crying by saying things like, "Why are you crying? No need to cry. Little Jessie wasn't crying!" With all the attention on crying, your little one will think their crying is the most impressive thing they did during the lesson.

Try saying things like: "Yes, you were nervous, but you were very brave, and I saw you put your eyes in the water three times!" "I saw you wanted to get out, but it's important to know how to swim, and I'm very proud of you for completing your lesson." "I saw you floating today, isn't it cool how the water holds you up?" The more you focus on the positive, the sooner the child will also focus on the positive.

AT THE LESSONS, SHOULD I SIT BY THE POOL OR GO INSIDE?

If you feel the most at peace by the pool, you're welcome to sit nearby. If you do so, it's best to look on with positive, calm energy. Your child will feel your confidence. If your child is turning to you on a continuous basis, if you watch from inside you will allow them to focus on a higher level. Thusly, I recommend for you to watch from a place where you can see the child but where the child can't see you. This autonomy allows your child to create a bond with the teacher. It also removes the temptation of being distracted by mommy/daddy/caregiver. For many kids, having a loved one near, but not being able to be held by the loved one, makes it harder for them to focus on the task at hand. It may take a few lessons, but your little one will soon be at peace with the process.

The most important thing is consistency. If you sit by the pool, do so every time. (Unless your child is distracted. Then, it is best to watch from inside, and continue to move inside for every lesson.)

Of course, every swim school is different, so be sure to ask the instructor for their preference.

SHOULD MY CHILD WEAR GOOGLES?

Goggles are a debatable topic, but bottom line, if you go about four to five lessons and your little one (over three-years-old) isn't opening their eyes under water, you can add goggles to help them learn to open their eyes under the water. Once they get a feel for opening their eyes underwater, be sure to practice without the goggles a few times each lesson, so they don't become dependent on them.

Also, if you're in a pool which is highly chlorinated or has a high salt water content, go ahead and add goggles if your child's eyes are sensitive or painful after swimming. Swimming should be fun and empowering, and there's nothing fun about painful eyes. However, if your child is under three, and your pool is mild, I encourage you to teach your child to swim without goggles. (If they were pushed into a pool unexpectedly, they would not be wearing goggles! So make sure they know how to swim without them as well as with them.)

DOES MY CHILD NEED TO WEAR SUNSCREEN?

Yes and no. Studies show about 20 minutes of sun exposure is good for us[22]. Sun, without sunscreen, gives us vitamin D. Of course, you don't want your little one to be out all day without protection, but if you aren't in the sun more than 20 minutes, try doing the lesson without sunscreen. (Unless your child has a medical condition or your common sense tells you otherwise.)

If your child will be in the sun longer than 20 minutes, be sure to put sunscreen on your child 30 minutes before they get into the pool. If you smother them in sunscreen right before they get in the water, it may not sink in and the sunscreen will drip into their eyes. Sunscreen is often what causes eye pain, not the water!

Also, many sunscreens may have harmful chemicals in them[23]. My favorite sunscreen is Blue Lizard Australian Sunscreen. Try getting a sunscreen without harsh chemicals to protect your little one.

CAN I PUT MY CHILD IN FLOATIES?

I recommend never using floaties unless you're on a boat or it's a safety issue. Floaties not only give everyone a false sense of security, but they also provide your little one the wrong idea of where their buoyancy center is. Their natural buoyancy center is in the middle of their body. Why would you want to make them feel like they float from their arms (water wings) or from their necks (the Otterroo)?

That said, if you're on vacation and your sanity and your child's safety is in question, put them in a floatie. But try to keep it to one which maintains their center of buoyancy in the natural place (around their chest). And always watch your little one in the pool, even if they have their floatie on.

MERMAID TIP: Floaties vs. no floaties

James and Alex started lessons at the same time. Both were three-years-old and both didn't like going under the water. James, however, had experienced plenty of "play" time in the pool using a center of buoyancy floatation device (the water wings with the center strap). He loved to jump in and kick in his floatie. James was comfortable on the step and walking "moon walk." Alex, on the other hand, didn't have any previous water experience.

The first lesson James already had water modulation (walking on the step, how his body works in the pool) nailed. Alex, on the other hand, gripped my arms on the step and would walk in a jerky, fearful fashion. Both didn't love going under the water, but by the end of the lesson they could both submerge for three seconds with proper breath control.

At the second lesson, James (after the proper warm up) began to open his eyes under the water. He immediately understood how to do a Floaty Magic (front float, eyes in, without moving his arms and legs). James could glide out and by the end of the lesson James was already on swimming. Alex, at the second lesson, was much more comfortable on the steps. He could put his face underwater, but he wasn't opening his eyes. He also was fearful in the water. Every time he would come out to me he would grip my arms.

Five lessons later, James is swimming, swimming with intention, and working on breaths. Alex, however, is still working on floats and glides. Because he had no water experience to pull from, his journey is a slightly slower one.

In conclusion, being in the water with a floatation device (as long as it keeps buoyancy in the center) facilitates children gaining valuable skills like propelling in the water, walking on the steps and becoming comfortable in the pool. Every child's path is different. Do what you feel is best for yours.

Once lessons begin, it's better to remove the floaties and not switch back and forth. Consistency is key.

SHOULD I GET MY CHILD A RASH GUARD?

If you're teaching your little one outside, rash guards are a great alternative to sunscreen. However, if the pool water is chilly I advise not to use rash guards. Rash guards keep your child colder in chilly weather because the rash guard becomes wet and doesn't allow the sun to warm your child's skin.

WHAT SHOULD THE POOL TEMPERATURE BE?

Ideally, the pool temp should be about 90 degrees. Little ones also lose body heat much faster than adults. Learning to swim is a new, challenging experience and if your little one is shaking and miserable it will be almost impossible to get them to relax. The more comfortable your little one is, the easier they will ease into swimming.

WHAT IF I DON'T HAVE A PRIVATE POOL THAT CAN BE HEATED?

If you're swimming at a public pool or community pool, try to pick a warm day outside, so your little one is comfortable. The more relaxed they are, the more seamless the experience will be.

MY CHILD TOOK A 10 LESSON INTENSIVE AND THE INSTRUCTOR TOLD ME MY CHILD DOESN'T NEED MORE LESSONS, IS THAT TRUE?

No! This is one of the most heartbreaking and dangerous things I've heard. Even if your child can swim, they must practice. Swimming, like all other sports, takes endurance and your child can become out of shape. Even if your child is athletic, swimming uses muscles other exercises do not.

Plus, swimming is a counter intuitive problem (see chapter 1) and they must practice. If you can't keep them in formal lessons, go ahead and take them to the pool yourself. There are activities in this book to guide you. It's imperative to keep your child in the water, working on their skills.

THE INSTRUCTOR SAID MY CHILD CAN SWIM, HOW CAN I TELL IF THEY ARE REALLY SWIMMING?

Can your child pop up for breaths? Can they jump in, turn, and swim to the wall? Can they swim across the pool without struggling? If they catch a mouthful, can they recover?

If you answered no to any of these questions, they are not Swim Safe*. If you answered yes to all those questions, great! But be sure to keep your little one practicing. As I mentioned previously, swimming is a counter intuitive problem, so the more they practice, the more likely they won't panic should they get in a scary situation.

HOW MANY TIMES A WEEK SHOULD MY CHILD SWIM?

Initially, the more back-to-back lessons your child can take the better. Many schools offer intensive or immersion programs where you swim eight to ten days in a row. This is the best way to get your little one swimming.

After the eight to ten days, it's best to keep lessons going at least two to three times a week for a swimmer who isn't Swim Safe yet. For swimmers who are Swim Safe, you can drop to once or twice a week (but again, the more practice the better. It doesn't have to be in a formal lesson, it can be with you).

Ideally, take an eight to ten day session, then spend a few weeks honing their skills learned. Then do another eight to ten day session. Repeat this process until your child is Swim Safe. (For a three-year-old becoming Swim Safe could take anywhere from one immersion to three immersions, depending on their personality, skills, and abilities.) The immersions are a great way to pass through each phase. The weekly lessons will hone their skills.

*ALWAYS WATCH YOUR CHILD IN THE POOL. Swim safe or not. It's never safe to have a swimmer swim alone.

5 LESSON PREPARATION TIPS:

You're motivated and ready to teach your little one. Great!
Gather the following items before you go to the pool. To make it easy
for you, I have all the links to these items at www.AMermaidsGuide.
com.

1) Toys. I like mermaids or fish. If you can, find some small rings and
a toy, like a dolphin, to be able to toss the rings onto. The rings should
float, and be small enough to carry comfortably.

2) Waterproof watch. This will help you monitor the time you spend in
the pool. Set a certain amount of time aside, and keep it manageable.
Twenty minutes is a perfect amount of time for most children. If your
little one is older, you can extend it to thirty. Learning to swim is both
physically and emotionally demanding. It's best to end before your
little one is fatigued so they complete their lesson on a positive note
instead of being exhausted and frustrated.

3) Swim Bag. To hold all of your items.

4) Towel, swimsuit, and swim diaper if needed. (You can find great re-
useable swim diapers on-line.)

5) Stickers. Stickers are great motivators. I encourage you **not** to
make the awards bigger...like offering a toy. Small tokens of their
achievement are plenty. Place the sticker on their hand after the lesson,
then (before the shower) add it to a piece of paper documenting their
sessions. A page of stickers is a great visual of their achievements.

AT THE POOL: Use the Golden Rules. If your child doesn't like
going to the pool, be the Buddha from the moment you broach the
subject with them. Be the Buddha, Mirror and Agree, AHM.

BEFORE you start, always remind your swimmer to ALWAYS SWIM WITH a grownup.

SAFETY FIRST: Safety during lessons is TOP priority. Keep your hands near your child at ALL times if the child cannot swim. Never move further away from the child than they can swim. For example: A techniques swimmer can swim the whole pool, so you can cross to the other side and have them swim to you. But with a new swimmer, who can't even put their face under yet, keep a hand on them at all times. For a swimmer who can glide, but not breathe, you can move away the distance they can go under the water comfortably. NEVER leave a child unattended in the pool. After the lesson, make sure the swimmer is safely out of the water. (If you're at a private pool, be sure to close the pool and lock the gate.)

CHAPTER 5:
10 Pool Exercises For Babies

Can babies learn to swim? A child at 12 months old can propel in the water from point A to B without assistance if given the time to learn how to do so. That said, toddlers won't swim with intention until 16-18 months. For most of us, we just want our babies to have a good head start for when they are ready to learn how to swim. Here are 10 exercises to do with your child in the pool to prepare them for their swim journeys.

1) STARTING POSITION

Hold your little one in your arms, your face level with theirs. Place your hands under their armpits, so their legs extend behind them in a prone position (legs are parallel to the pool floor).

Be sure their necks are strong enough to keep their faces from flopping into the pool. Move them back and forth. I like to say, "Ear in the water, ear in the water, ear in the water, weee!" You can take any song and sing it to them as you move them around.

My favorite is:

This is the way the Lady rides, trop trop trop

This is the way the Gentleman rides, clop clop clop

BUT this is the way the farmer rides, trippy trop trippy trop trippy trop!

WHAT IF MY CHILD CLINGS TO ME?

If your child likes to be close to you, start there. But, ideally, you want to move them out and away from you, so they get the feeling of being independent in the water. If you always hold them vertically on your hip or in your arms, you're not simulating a swimming position. Keep your expression confident and positive, even if your little one seems a little wary about the new experience. The calmer you are, the more they will enjoy it.

2) STANDING ON THE STEPS

Have your little one stand on whatever step they can stand on without having their face in the water. (Ideally, the water should be at chest level.)

For tiny babies, you may have to give them more support as you keep them stable on the step. But babies who are a little older, eight to twelve months, can often hold most of their weight on the step. Start by holding their bodies, and as they gain confidence, hold their hands instead. Pretty soon, your little one will be able to balance on the step by themselves. (Be sure, even if they can stand on their own, to keep your hands close.)

Walking on the step seems simple, but the more practice they have figuring out how their bodies work in the water, the better.

3) MOONWALK

Moonwalk is the same idea as standing on the step, but this time, let them walk from side to side. Start by holding their hand or bodies and then, as they gain confidence, ease off so they, eventually, can do it on their own. You can sing, "Moonwalk! Moonwalk!"

4) CHUGGA-CHUGGA

Go to the wall. Turn your child away from you and place your knee under your little one's butt. Then raise your hands on the wall and show them how to hold on. For the little ones, you may have to place your hands over the top of their hands so they get the idea. It's also prudent to set your hand on the wall in front of their faces in case they accidentally look down (you don't want them to bang their heads). Work with them to get the feeling of moving themselves along the wall. As they gain confidence, allow them to do it on their own.

5) BACK FLOAT

Some little ones don't mind the feeling of leaning back in the water. There are a few ways to do this, but I like to place the child facing away from me. Then I set one hand on their tummy and one hand on their lower back. I lower their head next to my ear and then I have them lean back onto my shoulder. I walk backwards and sing a little song.

As your little one gets more comfortable, you can do back floats without them resting their head on your shoulder. To do this, turn your child away from you and lower them, so your hands are cradling their head.

If your little one seems comfortable, you can slowly ease the amount of support and begin to let them feel the water holding them up.

Always follow the rhythm and energy of your baby. If they begin to fuss or become uncomfortable, move them into a different position and try again later.

6) BUBBLES, PUFFERFISH, AND HUMMMM

In the starting position, blow bubbles into the water. Start by blowing gently in your little one's face so they can feel the air coming out of your lips, and then lower your lips into the water. You may have to do this quite a few times. Just let them watch you perform the action and soak it in. Depending on the age of your child, they might imitate you right away!

The goal of teaching bubbles isn't to have your little one blow bubbles every time they submerge. The goal is to teach them how to control their breath and see how, when they blow out, air comes out. The exercise is also helpful to work on motion control. They have to be cognizant of their mouth placement as to not take a breath when their lips are under the water.

For Pufferfish, take a big "mouthful" of air, puff your cheeks out, and hold your breath. Say, "Pufferfish!" then take a "bite" of air and lower your face into the water. Pufferfish is all about your little one learning how to hold their breath. For submersions, you want your little one doing Pufferfish, not blowing bubbles.

If your little one is over two-years-old, and if they seem to be getting water in their mouth or up their nose during submersions, instead of having them blow bubbles through their mouth under the water, you want them to HUMMMM. (Humming through their nose will allow less air to escape, which will keep them buoyant and help them later in their swim journey.) To teach humming under the water, show them how to hum above the water, and then lower your nose under the water.

7) SUBMERSIONS

Even if your child isn't blowing bubbles, you can still teach them submersions. I like to demonstrate with a toy first. I take a toy and tell the toy we are going under the water on the count of three.

I demonstrate how the toy goes under the water several times before doing the exercise with the child.

When you're ready to do a submersion, hold your child in the start position, and tell them they are going under on three. Count one, two, three and then blow on their face right as you smoothly and slowly pull them under water towards you (don't dunk them straight down). The ideal path is a crescent just under the water surface. You can start by submerging part way. Just their face or even nose and mouth is okay. When they come up, be sure your face is confident and relaxed.

8) GLIDE OFF THE STEP

Once your little one can stand on the steps, you can begin gentle glides out to you. For information on glides move to the next chapter.

9) Humpty Dumpty

If your child can sit up and is comfortable going under the water, you can add a submersion from the edge of the pool. Have your child sit on the edge, then guide them gently into the water by their hands or using the holds described in chapter six.

10) Kickies and still

To teach your little one proper kick position, hold them in your arms with your hands under their legs. Their kicks should be tight, with small splashes. You can do the kicks for them at first, and then have them do it themselves.

It's essential for your child to know the water holds them up, but kickies make them go fast (you don't want your child thinking they have to kick to float). As you teach your little one kicks tell them, "The water holds you up, but kickies make you go fast!"

Try doing kicks, and then have them freeze with their legs behind them and say, "Still!" Being able to isolate their kicks will help with the next swimming phases. The most important thing, when swimming with your child, is to enjoy the experience. If you're having fun, chances are they will too.

CHAPTER 6: PHASE 1
FLOATS, GLIDES AND SUBMERSIONS

GETTING IN THE POOL

When you get to the water, square your shoulders; be calm and confident with your little one. Lock eyes with your child. Give them a moment. Smile. Tell them you're going to teach them to swim. Let them have a moment to connect with you. If they seem nervous, you can say, "I'm here to keep you safe. I promise." Be sure to set the intention of keeping them safe with meaning and love because they will be able to tell if you're faking it.

Get your toys out of your bag, and step onto the bottom step. Check your watch and note the start time. You have about twenty minutes (or however long you have set for yourself) once the child is in the pool. Be aware of the time, so the lessons are about the same length each day.

Once you are set, take your child by the hand and say, "We're going to come on the first step." Once they do that say, "Look, see! You already know how to do this!"

If they seem to be struggling to get into the pool, go to your child and use H2H and say, "You can walk to the pool, or I will pick you up. What would you like?"

If they don't answer, tell them you're going to pick them up and bring them into the pool. And then do so, calmly and deliberately. Once in, if they are crying or resisting, take them into the mid-shallow end. Hold them and use AHM and M&A. Then let them know what they have to do to get out of the pool. For example: "You want to get out, I see you want to get out. Yes, we'll get out. All we have to do is put the toys away, and then we can get out." Repeat this until the child calms down. If the child doesn't calm down and it feels like they aren't going to...proceed to the next step.

TOYS ON THE STEP

GOAL: Confidence building

AGES: All

HOW: (If child seems nervous) Look the swimmer in the eye, hold them securely (H2H) and say, "I'm here to keep you safe. You can do this. I will keep you safe, I promise. Take a toy and throw it on the top step."

For younger kids, keep hold of their hand or body and take a toy and throw it on the first step yourself. Then clap (or smile if your hands are busy holding them) and give yourself positive reinforcement.

Then give the child a toy to throw toward the first step. If they throw it too far, don't react. Just fetch it (keeping Safety First in mind) and give it back to them with a neutral expression. Then calmly say, "Throw the toy on the first step."

Continue until they place the toy on the first step, at which point you cheer. If your child is older, two and a half to five, the cheer can be more of a statement "You did it. You threw it on the first step." Repeat for at least three-five toys.

WHAT IF MY CHILD WON'T LISTEN?

Keep repeating. If the swimmer throws it into the pool, don't make a joke about it. Pick it up, without a reaction, and give it back to them. Repeat, "Throw the toy on the first step." For a particularly spirited child, this may take a few minutes. When they DO throw it on the first step clap and react positively.

WHAT IF THEY ARE SCREAMING AND WON'T LISTEN AT ALL?

If they continue to cry, move onto to the next exercise. With some children (if their amygdala is activated) you have to keep moving through the phases until their brain has a chance to relax into the experience. More on this in chapter 11.

MERMAID TIP: It's so easy!

Throwing toys on the first step seems really easy for older kids. The point is NOT to see if they can actually throw it on the first step, it's to set up:

A)   They have to listen.

B)   When you tell them to do something and they try, they have success!

STRUCTURE OF THE LESSONS

For the first five to ten lessons (and sometimes more) it's important to make a routine so the child knows there's a finite point to their lesson.

My lessons consist of "Putting the toys away" and "Playing the dolphin game."

PUTTING THE TOYS AWAY

For each activity in this book, choose a toy or (even better) let the student choose a toy.

1) Hold the toy up and ask, "Mr (or Mrs.) _____ (name of toy) what do you want to see?" then hold the toy to your ear as if you are listening. Nod, and say "_____ wants to see _____(activity) _____ (number of times)"

2) Take the toy with you as the child does the skill (you can tuck it into the bottom of your swimsuit, so you have your hands free). After the skill ask the toy if it was good (I hold the toy to my ear, and the toy "whispers" positive encouragement to me. After I react, I tell the child what the toy said).

3) Have the child "shake shake shake" all the water off the toy and put it on the side of the pool. For the younger kids, you can sing a little song, "Bye, bye (name of toy) Bye, bye (name of toy). Bye, bye (name of toy) we'll see you again next time!"

THE DOLPHIN GAME

Get a dolphin swim toy or any animal and light plastic rings.

1) Let the child choose a color of a ring and try to throw it on the dolphin's head. For beginning swimmers, this can just be for fun. They can even stay on the steps and toss the rings from there. If the swimmer is working on overcoming tears, you can help them place the ring on the dolphin. It's important to finish the dolphin game even if they are having a tough time with the lesson because it gives structure and also teaches them three main things:

o   They have to finish their lesson.

o   Crying doesn't get them out of trying.

o   When they try, they achieve.

Most of the time, children love the dolphin game. It's the last activity of the lesson, and kids usually relax into it. Try to make the dolphin game fun, so the end of the lesson ends on a high point.

2)   As they progress, the dolphin game is more challenging. Move away from the step and have them toss farther. If they miss, you choose an activity (like a glide, swim, or float) out to the ring. They can either scoop up the ring, and then you scoop them up, or they can scoop up the ring and then swim to you, depending on their level. Have them slam dunk the ring onto the dolphin. Then they (float, glide, or swim) back to the steps and choose another color.

o   Once they can do breaths, they can swim out, pick up the ring, take a breath, and then slam dunk.

o   When they are working on swimming with intention, they can swim to the ring, turn, and swim to you.

MERMAID TIP: Third person

Using toys is also a great way to have a "third person" so you and the student can be a team. If a child doesn't want to do the activity the toy suggests you can say, "But each toy needs a turn. We just need to put the toys away, play the dolphin game, and then we are all done!"

Toys are also a great way to get the kids in on the action. Let's say the swimmer doesn't want to put their face under. You can ask the toy how many times it wants to see their face go under the water. Have the toy say, for instance, "ten times!" and then ask the student if ten is too many. The student will say yes, so then you can ask the toy if it's okay if they just do it one time. Chances are the student will be so happy to only have to do one time, they will relax and complete the task at hand willingly. Keep mixing up the requests of the toys, but with the idea the child has to go under at least one time for each toy. You can also let the child choose how many times the toy wants to see it: one or three times?

INTRODUCTION EXERCISES / CONFIDENCE BUILDERS: MOONWALK

GOAL: Water awareness and confidence builders.

AGES: All

HOW: Pick a toy and ask it what it wants to see! It wants to see the Moonwalk. "We are going to do a Moonwalk. Hold my hand, I'll keep you safe the whole time, I promise." Hold their hand (or two hands for younger children) and have them walk along the step. The water should be chest level. If the child is nervous, you can start on the top step and then work down to the second or third step.

As you walk sing "Moonwalk, moonwalk, moonwalk." And when they reach one side clap and say "You did it." Or, for older kids ask, "Did you do it?"

As they get more confident, have them only hold one of your hands. Then, when they are ready, have them try it by themselves (be sure to keep your arms near them). Encourage them to feel the water on their fingers and hands. Let them discover what happens when they move their arms up and down. Ask them to try to hop like a bunny.

For swimmers ages two-and-a-half to three, this exercise should be relatively easy. Remind them to walk slowly. Use empowerment phrases such as, "You're in charge of the water. Move it out of your way."

BUBBLES: OVERRATED

Many swim schools spend a tremendous amount of time trying to teach the students to blow bubbles under the water. It's better to teach your little one how to hold their breath under the water.

I always tell my swimmers, "Keep your bubbles!" Why? Think of a helium balloon. It floats when it has helium in it, but when all the helium is out, it will sink. The same thing will happen with floating in the pool. If your little one blows all their air out, it will be harder to float.

The goal is to have them be able to take a breath and then control the "pressure" of the air in their bodies. This sounds more complicated than it actually is. Most kids do it naturally.

That said, it's okay to touch on bubbles as a skill in their tool box. Learning bubbles is more about controlling the timing of their breath. (See chapter 5 for more on this.)

Nose Bubbles

Nose bubbles are my favorite kind of bubbles. If your little one is getting water in their mouth or nose, this is the best way to overcome the problem.

GOAL: Keep water out of their mouth and nose

AGES: Two years and up

HOW: Ask the little one to hum above the water. Demonstrate and then have them try. Then say, "Humming is your super power against water in your nose! When you come out to me, go HUMMM under the water!" By blowing slowly out of their nose they can maintain the air in their lungs longer than if they push all the bubbles out of their mouth.

Chugga-Chugga

GOAL: Water awareness, pool safety

AGES: Twelve months and up

HOW: Go to the side of the pool. Place their hands on the edge. Say "BIG FINGERS!" Kids will often try to pull themselves up high on the wall. Encourage them to lower their shoulders into the water and say, "Let the water hold you up. I'm right here. I will keep you safe the whole time. I won't let you go." As you hold them, go lighter and lighter with your hands, but be sure to tell them what you are doing. Encourage a conversation. "Are you doing it?" "Look how cool! You're holding onto the wall!"

SUBMERSION INTRODUCTION: REACHING FOR TOYS ON THE STEPS

GOAL: Phase 1 (Working on submersions, eyes open, breath control.)
AGES: All
HOW: Have the swimmer take your hand and reach for a toy. Start with the toy at a level the swimmer doesn't have to go entirely under to reach it. Then clap when they get it!

Before every toy say, "You can go under water if you want to. It's cool! You can see underwater. It's like a superpower." and if they say no, just say, "Okay, when you're ready you can go under and surprise me."

Some children won't go under the water for the toys. If they don't, move onto GLIDES.

MERMAID TIP: BREATH TIMING

If they go under and catch a mouthful, cough along with them and use AHM. "Yucky! You drank some water. That tasted gross. Don't drink the water! Do like this (and then demonstrate Pufferfish)." Then move on with the lesson. At some point in your child's swim journey they will catch a little water in their mouth or down the wrong tube. Our bodies expel it naturally, by coughing, almost every time[24]. (For more info on this, read chapter 13). If you look nervous and worried when they accidentally take a mouthful, your little one will be scared to do it again. It's like riding a bike; they will fall off a few times before they get it. Encourage them to be independent and try. If they fail, they gain an opportunity to try again with adjustments. If the swimmer seems to be having trouble going under the water on the steps, move onto the next exercise. Submersions on the steps can be, for some kids, harder than glides because on the steps they have to not only control their breath, but they also have to manage their bodies. When they do introduction glides they only have to focus on their breath. So if your little one doesn't seem comfortable doing submersions on the steps, just move on. Once they understand proper breath control come back to this exercise.

GLIDES
STRAIGHT ARMS AND LEGS, ALLOWING THE WATER TO HOLD THEM UP

For swimmers over the age of two-and-a-half, glides and floats are imperative. After age two-and-a-half, their minds begin to anticipate fears, anxiety, and cause-and-effect. If your swimmer doesn't know how to float, and truly relax in the water, they can never be a strong, competent swimmer. The younger a swimmer learns how to float, the more ingrained into their bodies it becomes The most important part of glides is having the child FEEL the water hold them. The water holds them up, and kicks make them move.

For young swimmers, twelve months to two years, glides and kicks/swimming often happen congruently. Once gliding, the younger swimmer will naturally kick their legs. Allow this to happen for children under two-and-a-half or any swimmer not capable of isolating their movements. Before we go into glides, let's talk about...

THE COUNT

Anytime you are going to have your swimmer go underwater, tell your swimmer what they are going to do and then give them THE COUNT. One, two, three UNDER. Try to keep the pacing the same every time, so they know what to expect.

BABY GLIDES

GOAL: Phase 1 (relaxing in the water and breath control)
AGES: All
HOW: Tell them, "We are doing a baby glide." For kids who are nervous, state, "You won't go under water, I promise." (Again, if you promise something, you have to follow through. Don't ever put them under water if you say you aren't going to.)

Have your swimmer place their hands on your shoulders. Place your hands on their legs to keep them in a prone position. Then gently move back WITHOUT going under the water.

SERVER HOLD

On the way back to the steps, turn your swimmer away from you. Be sure to explain what you're doing. Place your left arm under their right armpit with your right arm holding their right leg so they are across your arms, flat as a pancake.

Once your swimmer gets the feel by doing baby glides, with their face out of the water, you're ready to do a submersion.

For submersions, start with the Child Control Hold. Your hands will be under their chest, and wrapped around their sides. Using the CCH (Child Control Hold) the swimmer can hold onto your arms as they go under. The child will feel secure and safe.

SUBMERSION

GOAL: Phase 1 (submersions)

AGES: All

HOW: Say, "On the count of three we are putting our eyes in the water." Count, and then go under on three. Remind them to take a big pufferfish breath. Start by only having them go under for a moment, and then, as they grow more comfortable, extend the time under the water. You may spend an entire lesson only going under for one second while they get used to it. It takes time to build up their breath control, so take it slowly.

Before you count, be sure to keep your expression positive. After the child goes under, use AHM. Don't assume your swimmer will not like the experience; it's pretty amazing to be able to go under. Be the Buddha, and read their emotion. If they seem a little stunned just say, "Oh, that felt a little funny! You went under the water!" If they cry and wipe their eyes say, "Oooo, the water tickles your eyes. It does feel funny. But you can do it!" and then move on. If you treat going under like it's a big deal, they will think it is. Going under water is amazing, but it's not epic.

Once your swimmer can hold their breath using the CCH, it's time to move to the Teacher Control Hold (TCH). The TCH hold gives you full control of their movement and will allow the water to start holding them up. To do the TCH, place your hands on the outside of their shoulders. Your thumb is around the front of their arm, and your fingers are outstretched, controlling the swimmer's body.

For swimmers who like to control the situation (more in chapter 11) TCH may feel uncomfortable. If they resist, use AHM, Mirror and Agree, and then get them in on the action by asking how many times they want to stay in this "tricky" hold. Most swimmers, however, don't mind. Don't anticipate them having any qualms with TCH, but be ready if they do. Start small, give The Count and then do a tiny submersion. Pick another toy and do it again.

Once they are comfortable with one second under the water, extend the submersion to two seconds. Then to three seconds. Once they can go three to five seconds with proper breath control, you can start working on releases.

RELEASES

Tell your child the water is going to hold them up. Say, "I'll hold you, then the water will hold you, and then I'll hold you!" At the start of releases, hold them the whole time, but allow your grip to be light in the middle of the submersion so the swimmer can start to feel the water holding them up.

After a few times practicing, let the water hold them up a tiny bit more. Don't rush this process; you want it to be natural so the child will trust the water.

Once you can feel them relaxing on the way out to you, in the middle, allow the water to hold them up for a second. Keep your hands close to their bodies; you're just releasing your grip. It's like flying!

BASKETBALL HOLD

Place one hand under the swimmer's armpit near you and the other under their bottom. Use the front hand to guide (much like a basketball shot) and the back hand to gently push them to the stairs. Be sure to keep your hands on the swimmer if they are new to the Basketball Hold. Give them more freedom once you feel their bodies relax.

If your swimmer is closing their eyes, be careful as you glide them toward the step. You may have to use a hand to block the stair, so they don't bump their head. Also, encourage them to keep their hands in front of them so they can catch themselves on the step.

MERMAID TIP: Submersions

KEEP SUBMERSIONS SLOW AND GENTLE. Give them a count, and go under slowly and gently.

Being the Buddha with submersions is key. Kids are excellent mind readers; they pick up on the tiny muscles in your face, which give away your real emotions. When your child looks to you before going under the water, it's imperative your face be reassuring, calm, and confident.

BIG GLIDES

Once your little one is comfortable with your hands releasing them for five seconds, they are ready for big glides.

For big glides use the Teacher Control Hold. Give your swimmer a count, then tilt them into a prone position and gently pull them toward you. Release their arms and allow the water to move them out to you.

Or, if your swimmer is ready, have them slowly push off the step and glide out to you.

For young kids who are unable to isolate and glide with straight arms and legs, let them kick on the way out to you. Then, later, teach them glides when they are capable of isolation.

For kids ages two-and-a-half and up, start every lesson with five or more perfect slow glides as a warm-up. Let them feel the water hold them up and allow the momentum to propel them forward. Then glide them back to the stairs using the basketball hold.

How do I know if my child is holding their breath?

As your child extends their submersions, here are some keys to know if they mistimed their breath and you should scoop them up immediately
.

4 Essential Scoop Signs

1) If you see a huge burst of bubbles from their mouth.

2) If there's a shift in the swimmer's movements. For example, if they are swimming normally and start to swim frantically. Or if they are swimming normally and suddenly go still. (Unless your child likes to stop and float. Then, obviously, this is fine.)

3) If they begin to shake their head back and forth like they are saying "NOOOO." This is usually a sign they are almost out of air. For some kids, they shake their heads when they start submersions. They do this because they feel like they are out of air, even if they aren't[25]. Keep working on small submersions, and as they get used to the feeling of holding their breath, the head shaking will go away. In the meantime, ignore the head shaking. If you comment on it, they will become aware of it and may do it even more. If you keep moving through the submersion series it will, eventually, go away.

4) Anytime you feel they didn't get a good breath, scoop them up. Watch for their inhale before they go under the water. If they seem to get a nice big breath, allow the glide to go a little longer. If they mistime the breath, scoop them up earlier.

Floatie Magics

GOAL: Phase 1 (Relaxation and breath control)
AGES: Two-and-a-half and up (Note: The swimmer must be comfortable going under water and holding their breath for three to five seconds before working on floatie magic. If your swimmer isn't

comfortable with submersions yet, work on the glides, and extending their breath control before trying Floatie Magics.)

HOW: Move away from the stairs. Place your hands in a CCH (Child Control Hold). The first time have them place their face in the water for ONE second. Tell them "I will not let you go. Place your eyes in the water for one second."

Then have them place their face for two seconds, then three. When they can go under for at least three seconds start to allow the water to hold them up by relaxing your grip on their body. Move your hands to their stomach. Tell them to raise their arms off of your arms and remind them the water will hold them up. Slowly release your grip and allow the water to hold them up. If you have a nervous swimmer, tell them your hands will be on them at all times, but your fingers will be light. Demonstrate your fingers tapping their tummy, lightly. Then have them place their face in the water, allow the water to lift them off your hands, but touch their bellies gently to assure them you're close.

Floatie Magics are the crux of Relaxation Based Swimming. The more relaxed your swimmers are on their Floatie Magics, the easier all the other phases will be.

Trouble shooting: Eyes closed
5 Easy Mermaid Tips

You can't force your child to open their eyes under water. Keep using Positive Affirmations to layer in their *desire* to see under the water. From the very first lesson, use empowerment phrases like, "Isn't it so cool you can see in the water? It's like having superpower!"

Many kids will have a natural curiosity about opening their eyes in the water, but some do not. If they don't open their eyes right away, try these techniques.

How Many Fingers

You can do this activity for any child over three. Have the swimmer place their face in the water, then hold out a certain number of fingers under the water. Have them tell you how many fingers you were holding up.

Fishing For Toys

Have the toys on the step. Hold a toy in your hand and tell the swimmer it's going to move around so they will have to open their eyes to find it.

Surprise me!

Have the swimmer glide out to you and say, "I think this time you're going to surprise me by opening your eyes!" When they do, put on a big "show" of being surprised.

Blink, Blink, Blink

Have the swimmer do a floatie magic or glide and tell them they don't have to open their eyes…they just have to, "blink, blink, blink" under the water. Demonstrate opening and closing your eyes quickly. "Blink, blink,

blink!'"

GOGGLES

If you spend more than five lessons and your child still won't open their eyes under the water, you can have them try with goggles on. Sometimes, just by opening their eyes under the water, even with goggles on, it will click with them that they can see under the water! (Note: If you do add goggles on, just be sure to have them practice without goggles every once in a while, so they don't become reliant on the goggles.)

BREATH EXPANSION

GOAL: Relaxation
AGES: 18 months plus
HOW: Skip to page 100 and follow the instructions for Swim Circles.

Often children aren't relaxed in the water because holding their breath is a new and uncomfortable experience[25]. Be sure to work on submersions. Start by having them go under for one second and then continue to expand their breath control until they can hold their breath at least five seconds. Most swimmers will be able to hold their breath for ten seconds, or even more, eventually. Swim Circles are a great way to exercise their "breath control" muscles.

PHASE 1: 4 KEY BATHTUB EXERCISES

1) Submersions in the bath tub. Have the child look for toys under the water with their eyes open and mouth closed like Pufferfish.

2) Pour water over their head (see chapter 3).

3) Breath Up, Pufferfish down (see chapter 3).

4) Kickies and Still (see chapter 3).

PHASE 1: 4 KEY REVIEW ITEMS

You will need to re-introduce each of these exercises every time you take your child swimming. These exercises are warm-ups. (You wouldn't ask a gymnast to perform her hardest moves without a proper warm up, in the same way, give your child's body a warm-up before moving onto harder tasks.) Even if your child is past phase one, it's best to re-introduce each of these exercises **every time** they swim.

1) Start with a small one-second submersion using Child Control Hold or Teacher Control Hold.

2) Extend the submersions to two, three, four and then five seconds. You can also add on Swim Circles (see chapter 8). Let their lungs warm up and "expand." Make sure they feel relaxed under the water for at least five seconds before doing floats and glides.

3) Baby glides and then big glides

4) Floatie Magics

Chapter 7: Phase 2
Swimming &
Swimming with Intention

SWIMMING:

There are two types of swimming: swimming, and swimming with intention. Swimming with intention is key to having a child who is pool and Swim Safe.

WHAT IS SWIMMING?

Swimming is moving from point A to point B *without* momentum helping them. If the swimmer is jumping into the water and using the momentum to propel them forward (even if they are "kicking" their legs) they are not swimming.

WHAT IS SWIMMING WITH INTENTION?

Swimming with intention is being able to hold your breath properly and swim from point A to point B, even if point A and B are not in a straight line. In order to swim with intention, the swimmers must know how to turn in the water, hold their breath, and propel properly. Not only must they understand the physical aspects of swimming, but must also grasp the mental aspects. The swimmer must be able to problem solve under the water. If your child fell in a pool, could they turn and grab the edge? If they fell off the step, could they do a U turn and make it back to safety?

KICKIES

GOAL: Phase 2 (propelling)

AGE: All

HOW: Have the swimmer place their hands on your shoulders, legs outstretched. Place your hands on their legs and help them get the feel of nice tight, small kicks. You can say, "splash, splash, splash!"

As the swimmer gets more comfortable with the position of kicks, allow your hands to release and have them hold their body in the correct position and kick on their own.

GLIDES WITH KICKS

Once your child can glide out to you nice and easy, go ahead and have them glide out and then tell them to "Kick, kick, kick!" Keep practicing back and forth from the step. On the way back to the step, use the basketball hold, and give them a little push so they can make it. Right now, it's about having them feel what it's like to move through the water while kicking, and not so much about the success and efficiency of the kicks.

Pizza Arms

GOAL: Phase 2 (Propelling)

AGE: 2 and up

We teach breaststroke arms instead of free style arms to start because breaststroke arms are smoother and calmer than freestyle arms. Breaststroke arms also help the child prepare to pop up for breaths in the next phase. There's no point in having your child do perfect freestyle arms without being able to take breaths or save themselves if they fall in. Save the flashy strokes for later.

HOW: Place the child on the step, or sit them on your lap on the steps. Place their hands together and extend them as from their chest out as far as you can. ("Cut the Pizza")

Flip their hands so the back of the hands are together. ("Thumbs in the sauce") Then have them push the water out to the sides. ("Spread the Sauce!")

If your child doesn't like pizza, you can cut the pie or the cake. "Cut the cake, thumbs in the frosting, spread the frosting."

The point of breaststroke arms isn't to have the perfect breaststroke formation. The point is to move from point A to point B safely and effectively. For younger swimmers, remind them to "Push the water out of the way." I even sometimes simplify it to, "reach and push!"

You can also say:

~ "Push the water behind you!"
~ "You're the boss of the water, move it out of your way."
~ "EXCUSE ME, Mr. Water! Out of my way!"

> **MERMAID TIP: Moving under the water**
> Each child is different. If your swimmer isn't moving their arms, but has excellent kicks, that's okay. Focus on their strengths. If they have good pizza arms, but their kicks aren't effective, just have them focus on their arms. If you give them too many things to think about at once, they will become overwhelmed[26]. Utilize their most efficient skills.

Tag

GOAL: Phase 2 (Propelling)
AGE: ALL
HOW: Hold the child out, say, "We're going to play tag. We're going to do a floatie magic and then you can try to catch me."

Place them close to you at first so they are able to kick and reach you fairly easily. When they get you, cheer! Now have them do another floatie magic, and this time step back slightly farther and have them catch you. Having your child propel from a stationary position will teach them how to move in the water.

TAG

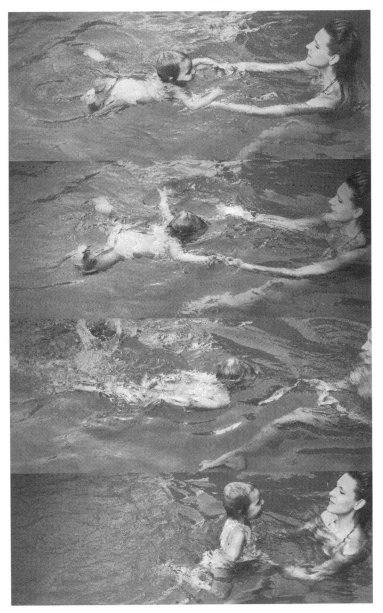

When playing TAG, it's best to give your swimmer a focal point. After you release them, place your hands a few inches below the surface of the water. Try not to move your hands once you place them for your swimmer's focal point.

If your child seems nervous, let them know you'll scoop them up after three seconds. I like to count under the water with my fingers so they have a visual of how long until you scoop them up. If you say you'll scoop them up in three seconds, be sure to scoop them up! (And always watch for the SCOOP SIGNS.)

SWIM TO THE STAIRS

Place the swimmer in the water near the stairs using the Server Hold (Page 68). Allow the water to hold them up and tell them *they* will have to use their kickies to make it to the steps.

As the child gets more comfortable, you can move further back. It's always harder to swim to the stairs, so start much closer to the steps than you think you will need to.

SWIM TO THE WALL

Swimming to the wall seems like it should be easy, but the wall seems very high to your little swimmer. The key to teaching them how to swim to the wall is to break it down into phases.

Start by holding them in the Basketball Hold at about a 45 degree angle to the wall. Explain the task at hand, "You are going to swim to the wall. I will hold you the whole time."

Then, gently glide them toward the wall and have them reach up and get it.

Hold them the whole time the first few times, but then allow them to "fall off the wall" and reach up by themselves to get back "on the wall." Practice falling off the wall, and then reaching back up to the wall a few times in a row before moving on.

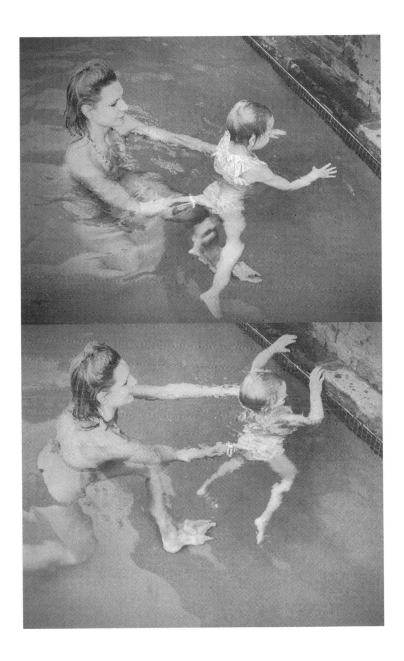

Then, slowly move them a tiny bit farther from the wall and then glide them up to it, releasing your grip but keeping your hand near them. Then, move a tiny bit farther back and release your grip a bit more. If your child seems nervous, tell them to reach for the wall and you will scoop them up after a certain number of seconds. Pretty soon your little one will be able to glide to the wall and reach up from two or three feet away.

TROUBLESHOOTING

My little one is still having trouble reaching up to the wall! What should I do?

TOES TO TUMMY

Toes to Tummy is a good way to help your swimmer get extra strength and ability to reach up high. Hold your little one out in front of you – have them pull their toes into your tummy.

Once they can do that, move back to the wall. Start close, have your little one reach up to the wall and tell them to pull their toes to touch the wall.

MY LITTLE ONE'S KICKS KEEP DROPPING, IT'S ALMOST LIKE THEY ARE CYCLING UNDER THE WATER. WHAT SHOULD I DO?

It's normal for your little one to have their kicks lower and raise as they go through the process of learning to swim. If your little one does more than two swims with their kicks dropped, try one of these exercises to get your swimmer back into the proper position.

TOY GRAB

This is the most effective way to get your little one's kicks back in place. Have them choose a toy. Then place the toy in your hands at about a 45 degree angle down in the water.

Tell your little one to try to grab the toy. By placing a toy under their natural eye line you give them a focal point. It makes them reach **down**, which, in turn, pops their kicks **UP**!

It's more effective to use physical triggers vs *telling* them what to do.

BRACING

Use TCH (Teacher Control Hold) and angle their body slightly down as they swim. Alternate between Bracing and regular swimming. Soon, their kicks will be up again!

POP THE HIPS

For younger kids you can also pop their hips up as they swim to you by reaching over them, gently pulling up on their hips to get their legs back up and behind them.

KICKIES

Place the swimmer's hands on your shoulders, put your arms under their legs and keep their legs up on top of the water. Make their legs go "Splash, splash, splash" on top of the water and remind them "KICKIES UP UP UP to GO GO GO." Then lower their kicks down to a vertical position and say, "Kickies down make you stop." Finally, raise their kicks back up again and say, "Kickies up make you go!"

SPIN, SPIN, SPIN

GOAL: Phase 2 (Swimming with intention)
AGE: All
HOW: Have the swimmer face away from you. Tell them they can spin in the water. Take their hands and push the water around to demonstrate with their face above the water.

Then place your hands under their armpits and face them away from you. Tell your child you will put them under the water and they should spin like a top (or ballerina) to you. "Spin, Spin, Spin!"

The first several times give them a little momentum on the spin by gently guiding their bodies with your hands. (Photo above) This will give them the feel of spinning and how to move their arms to make it happen.

As they get comfortable with spinning, do less and less with the amount of help you're giving them. Then, have them swim farther. Assure the nervous swimmers, you will scoop them up after a certain number of seconds, even if they don't get to you.

Spin, Spin, Spin is one of the most important exercises you can do with your little one. By assuring they know how to spin and swim to you, you're helping them learn how to swim with intention.

U-Turn

GOAL: Phase 2 (Swimming with intention)

AGES: All

HOW: Sit with your swimmer on the step with both of you facing the pool. Tell your swimmer to jump out and then swim back to the step. The first time, have them push off like they are doing a glide, then gently turn their body for them to guide them back to the step. (Use the same "guiding hand positions" as Spin, Spin, Spin.) Repeat with less and less guidance until they can jump in and turn back to the top step without help.

Pool Safety Preparation

Jump in, turn, and swim to safety.

1) SWIMMING TO THE WALL: Start close to the wall to build their confidence. Then move farther away in small intervals as the swimmer gains confidence.

2) SPIN AND GRAB: Start close to the side of the wall with your swimmer facing away from the wall. Tell the swimmer to Spin, Spin, Spin and grab the wall.

3) ELBOW, ELBOW, TUMMY, LEG, LEG: Now that your swimmer can grab the wall, they need to know how to climb up and out to safety.

Teach your little one to put their elbow up, then their other elbow.

Now PULL their tummy up.

Next, one leg and then the other leg.

You'll have to help them the first few times, but soon they will get the hang of it.

4) HUMPTY DUMPTY: Start by having your child sit on the edge of the pool. Use the TCH and slowly lower them into the water. Then, help their bodies turn and reach up to grab the wall. The first time you do this, keep your hands on the swimmer at all times. Use the same type of gentle assistance as you did when you were teaching Spin, Spin, Spin and U-turn. As your little one gets more confident, you can gently assist them into the water and then allow them to do the second part (Spin and Grab) by themselves.

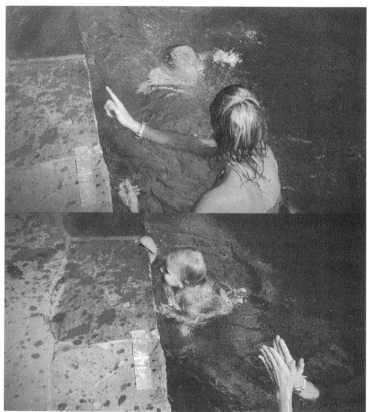

5) JUMPING FROM THE WALL. First, when they are standing on the edge, tell them they always have to ask a grown up before they go swimming. It's always a good idea, especially for younger swimmers, to make sure this is implemented and habitual.

CHILD: "May I jump in the pool?"

YOU: "Yes you may, far away." The first time they jump, either hold their hand or their arms and help them jump away from the pool wall. Then, assist them turning and getting back to the edge.

As they get more comfortable, it's time to let them jump on their own. But before you do, explain why they must jump away from the wall. I like to demonstrate what will happen if they jump too close by taking a toy fish and having it jump too close and "bonk" its head on the wall.

Even if you think they have a handle on it, it's always better to be on the safe side. Stand perpendicular to the wall and place one hand behind the swimmer to use as a "safety rail" in case they don't jump out far enough. Use this hand to push them farther out if need be. Use the other hand in front, as a "target" to show them where to jump, or to hold your swimmer's hand with your second hand.

Once your swimmer can jump from the side, turn, and swim back to the wall, they are ready for a pool safety test!

POOL SAFETY TEST

Go out of the pool with the swimmer. Place their toes on the edge. Tell the swimmer they are going to jump into the water, turn and swim to the edge.

If the student is scared do H2H, look them in the eye and tell them, "You can do it." have them repeat "I can do it." On the first "jump" gently lower them in, close to the edge.

Then, kneel down so you can make eye contact with them if they look up at you. Watch as they turn and swim back.

Once they master that, have them jump slightly farther out. And then a little farther. Soon they will be able to jump out, turn and swim back on their own. Be sure to watch for the Scoop Signs. You may have to give them a hand if they mistime a breath or jump too far. Remind them it's okay, and let them try again. If they don't get to the wall on their own more than two times in a row, take a step back to the previous activity. They may need more of a build up, and you don't want to create a habit of you reaching down to assist them. The goal is for them to have independence and know if they fell in they could turn, swim to the wall, and save themselves.

Once a child can jump in, turn, and swim to the edge they have completed the first level of pool safety. Now it's time to make them SWIM SAFE by adding on PHASE 3 (breaths).

PHASE 2: 5 ADDED REVIEW ITEMS

You will need to re-introduce each of these exercises every time you take your child swimming. The first 4 items are from phase 1. Be sure to review those FIRST, before adding on the phase 2 items.

PHASE 1 REVIEW

1) Start with small one-second submersions using Child Control Hold or Teacher Control Hold.

2) Extend the submersions to 2, 3, 4 and then 5 seconds. You can also add on Swim Circles (see chapter 8). Let their lungs warm up and "expand." Make sure they feel relaxed under the water for at least five seconds before doing floats and glides.

3) Glides

4) Floatie Magics

PHASE 2 REVIEW

1) Tag

2) Swimming to and from the steps

3) Spin, Spin, Spin

4) U-turn

5) Jump, turn, and swim to the edge

CHAPTER 8: Phase 3
Breaths

Being able to pop up for breaths is a crucial step to having a Swim Safe swimmer.

Breathing is something your child has been doing their whole life, but chances are swimming is the first time they will have to *think* about breathing[27]. So far, in phase one, they learned to hold their breath. Now they have to learn how to exhale and inhale, all while pushing their faces up and out of the water. Popping up for breaths is one of the harder aspects of learning how to swim.

In order to pop up for breaths, four factors are in play:

1)   Physical strength
2)   Timing
3)   Relaxation
4)   Mental toughness/bravery

For children under two, breaths can be tricky. They don't have the strength and coordination of older children. But with patience and perseverance, children as young as nineteen months can learn how to pop up and take breaths.

Be patient and layer in an accumulation of all the exercises in this chapter while teaching breaths. It will be the accumulation of all the activities which will give your swimmer the tools needed to pop up for air.

SWIM CIRCLE

GOAL: Phase 3 (relaxation, timing, and breath expansion)
AGE: All
HOW: Hold the swimmer in TCH (Teacher Control Hold), and have them glide or kick to you while you hold them. Walk backwards, in a circle, and when they need a breath they will naturally look up to the sky. Demonstrate how to take only one breath above the water.

Swim Circles, Breath Expanding Swim Circles, and Floatie Magics are the cornerstones of Relaxation Based Swimming. I start working Swim Circles as early as phase one.

At the beginning, you can rotate their bodies back to help get them into the right breath position and get their faces up and out of the water.

As they improve, try to keep your hands at the same level under the water, forcing the swimmer to push against your hands and tilt their faces upward. As they gain confidence, you can angle them slightly down in the water. By adding resistance to their movement, when you release them to try on their own, they will have the muscles built up and it will feel "easy" to lean back and get the breath.

*= Breath

Why is it called a Swim Circle? In this drawing, you'll see the overhead view of your movement. As your child gets breaths, keep walking backwards in a circle. When you arrive back at the step, let your little one have a rest.

MERMAID TIP: Shouldn't they blow out under the water and then come up for air?

Yes, eventually. Bodies are amazing; they will naturally figure out the easiest way to do things[28]. (It's similar to why exercises become less effective over time. Our system is trained to conserve energy and discover the easiest way to do things.)

If you over-explain breaths, the swimmer will start to over-think the process and tense up. Breaths are natural. When your little one pops up for air, they will usually exhale first, and then take in new air. Most of the time you don't even have to say anything.

If your little one isn't exhaling, try having them say a funny word when they come up for a breath. Tell them to scare you and say, "BOO!"

(By saying the word they will naturally exhale and then inhale before they go back under the water.) Slow the process down if need be. Have them blow OUT and breath IN and then go back under. Eventually, they will naturally begin to exhale under the water before they come up. Blowing out under water is something they will learn through practice, not by explanation.

BREATH EXPANDING SWIM CIRCLES

Have your little one go under for four seconds, and then have them come up for air. Then challenge them to go under for five seconds, and then lift them up for a breath. Then see if they can go six seconds, get a breath, and back under for seven seconds. Then see if they can go under for eight seconds. (But remember, safety first.)

> **MERMAID TIP: Control the breath, control the body**
> Your breath, mind and body are all connected[29]. The connection is one of the reasons Yoga is so popular. If you can control your breathing, you can control your body. Swim Circles are a great way to relax your child. I use swim circles when I feel the child is getting anxious. Swim Circles are, after all, anxiety free! I'm holding them the whole time, and all they have to do is look up for a breath whenever they need it. By having them hold their breath for three to five seconds, look up and take a deep breath, and then go back under, they are naturally doing meditative breathing.

CRAZY KOO-KOO BIRD

GOAL: Phase 3 (timing of the breath)
AGES: Two and up
HOW: Hold the swimmer's hands as they swim, allow them to push down on your hands to pop their heads up for a breath.

Try to keep your hands at an even level so the swimmer is pushing against your hands in order to look up. Try not to raise them up, let them push against your hands. As your swimmer gets more confident, you can open your hands so they are just pushing against your palm. The stronger they get, the more you can lower your hands when they push against your hands, causing them to do more of the work.

Remind them to LOOK UP for a breath. "Breathe UP to the sky!" At first, the swimmer may take a full second or two to take a breath. Practice slowly at first so they have a moment to time out their breaths. Ideally, you want them to pop up, take a nice quick, clean breath, and then go back under. With practice, they will be able to reach out, push the water down, and pop up on their own.

MERMAID TIP: My tummy hurts

If your swimmer complains of a tummy ache they are probably swallowing air as they pop up and go back underwater. They may have gas or burp a lot[30]. Be aware of their physical state and modulate the number of times you work on breaths.

COBRA

GOAL: Phase 3 (strength needed to take a breath)

~ Cobra is a great way to strengthen the swimmer's back and arms. It also helps them feel how to arch toward the sky to take a breath. Some swimmers find this position uncomfortable, but try to keep it fun and have them work on it a few times each session. (Unless, of course, there's a medical reason not to!)

AGES: Nineteen months and up

HOW: Turn the swimmer away from you, facing the step. Tell the swimmer you are right behind them and will help them with a breath in the middle. Point to where the middle is (between you and the step) and when they get to the middle you can choose a "PICK POINT."

3 PICK POINTS

1) Easiest: Hips. Place your hands on each side of their hips and tilt their bodies so their face angles up to the sky. This is the easiest pick point because you're creating the most support, and they are doing the least amount of muscle work.

2) Mid-level: Knees. Place your hands midway on their legs. Hold their legs behind them and have them push the water down (doggy paddle style) to arch up and get their face out of the water.

3) Advanced: Feet. This will make them use the most muscles to be able to arch back and get their face out of the water. This pose will also force them to push down on the water with their hands because you have taken their legs out of the equation.

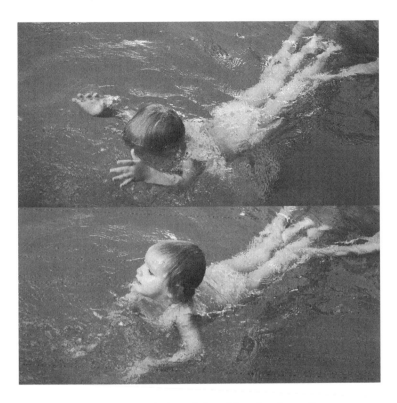

You can do a variation of the pick point depending on your swimmer's level and body type. As they push the water down, remind them to look up to the sky. Once you hear a nice breath, release them back to the water and have them finish the swim to the wall/steps.

Cobra pairs well with Crazy Koo-Koo Bird. Combine the exercises by having the child do Crazy Koo-Koo Bird away from the steps, and Cobra back to the steps.

COBRA AND SPIN

GOAL: Phase 3 (strength and mental toughness)

AGES: Two years and up

HOW: Start the swimmer facing away from you, glide them out while keeping hold of their feet or hips. Have them look up and push the water down to get a breath (Cobra). Then, release their legs and have them Spin, Spin, Spin and swim to your hands.

By combining Cobra with Spin, Spin, Spin, you are simulating what would happen if they were to fall in the pool. Be sure to use the same incremental teaching as you did when teaching Spin Spin Spin (guide their bodies the first few times).

DEEP SEA DIVING

GOAL: Phase 3 (breath timing)

~Deep sea diving is useful in several ways. First of all, it's fun for the swimmer to feel the water popping them up, which, in turn, often makes them even more of a relaxed swimmer. It's also an excellent way to practice breath timing.

AGES: 18 months and up

HOW: Place a toy at the bottom of the pool. The toys should be shallow enough so you can hold the swimmer's hand the entire swim to the bottom of the pool.

Stand on their left side. Place your right hand on their back and your left hand on their left hand (or vice versa if you're left-handed). Your left hand serves as a guide, and the right hand is going to do the pushing. It's similar to the Basketball Hold, but you'll be gliding them down instead of on top of the water.

The first time, give them The Count and then gently push them down about six inches under the water. Allow the water to lift them up, but keep your hands on them. You can ask them:

YOU: "Did you get the toy?"
CHILD: "No."
YOU: "It's okay, let's try again!"

The second time push them a little lower in the water. Ask them the same series of questions. The third time they should be pretty close to the toy at the bottom. If they don't get it, ask them if they want to try again. Usually, by this point, they are excited to try again.

MERMAID TIP: Deep sea diving is a microcosm for life
Deep sea diving is one of my favorite activities. It's like a microcosm for life. Usually, the swimmers start out and they don't want to try. It's scary to think about going to the bottom of the pool. Why would they want to try that? But, by assuring them they are going to be safe, they try. The first time they don't succeed, but they discover diving down is not as scary as they initially thought.
The second time, the swimmer is usually much more likely to be excited about the challenge at hand. Even if they try again, and they still don't get the toy, what a great way to teach them to keep trying.

(Note: Since you are the one controlling how close they are to getting the toy, be sure to have them dive deeper in small increments.) By the third or fourth time, you can push them low enough to grab the toy. When they get it, their faces light up with delight. Something that, moments before, seemed insurmountable, has been conquered!

DEEP SEA DIVING WITH A BREATH

GOAL: Phase 3 (Timing, strength, relaxation)

AGES: 18 months and up

HOW: Once your little one can get the toy holding your hand, let them know you'll be letting the water hold them up. If they get nervous, use H2H.

Use the same hand position as deep sea diving on the way down, and then, once they are part way down, release your guiding hand. Be sure not to push too hard. (You don't want them to smack their head on the bottom of the pool!). It's better to start too soft with the push than too hard. You'll figure out how much force you need to exert in order to get them at the right level to grab the toy.

Let the water lift the child back to the top. Most of the time the water lifts the child easily. If your little one doesn't pop up, remind them to take a big breath before they go down.

This is a great exercise for swimmers who are beginning with breaths because they use the momentum of the water to help them pop up and get a breath after they grab the toy at the bottom.

FLOATIE-POPS

GOAL: Phase 3 (Combination of strength and timing)

AGE: Two-and-a-half and up

HOW: Have the swimmer do a Floatie Magic, then count to three (underwater with your fingers) and have them push the water down and look to the sky and say "POP!"

Note: For swimmers over two-and-a-half years old, sometimes they can do breaths right away. To do Floatie-Pops, your swimmer must be able to do a perfect Floatie Magic. If your swimmer doesn't understand how to isolate their arms and legs, just skip this exercise and work on the other exercises in this chapter.

Chances are, when they first start, your child will time it out enough to say "Pop" and not take a breath after they say it. Scoop them up when they go back under the water so they don't inhale under the water. Once they are good at saying, "Pop," show them how to take a breath at the top instead of saying the word. Have them do Floatie Magic, and then look up and take a breath, and then back to Floatie Magic.

MERMAID TIP: Nervous breathing
Some swimmers have "nervous breathing." Nervous breathing is a series of short, shallow inhales and exhales instead of one big, relaxed breath. If your swimmer does nervous breathing, have them practice Swim Circles.

My Turn, Your Turn

GOAL: Phase 3 (endurance and breaths)
~ My Turn, Your Turn is a great exercise once your little one can pop up for a single breath. By alternating with them as they swim across the pool they will practice popping up on their own, but they won't get tense or nervous because they know you'll help them with the next breath.
AGE: eighteen months and up
HOW: Tell the swimmer they will take the first breath and you will help them with the second breath. On their turn, move your hands out of the water. Then, on your turn, place your hands under the water so they know you'll help them. Then raise your hands out of the water when it's their turn.

After they have mastered taking every other breath, you can change it to every third breath. Say, "You get the first two breaths, and then I'll help you with the third breath."

MERMAID TIP: Not taking complete breaths
If your child doesn't take a full breath when it's their turn, it's okay. Make sure they get a nice relaxed breath when it's *your* turn, and eventually they will connect the dots and take a relaxed breath when it is their turn.

LAPS

GOAL: Phase 3 (endurance)

AGE: Two years and up

HOW: Once your child can take breaths, have them practice some laps. Start with a short distance. Stay in front of your swimmer and be sure to keep a calm, positive expression as they swim across. Remind them to swim slowly and let the water hold them up. If they get stuck, scoop them up. If they get stuck two times in a row, do one of the previous exercises so they don't lose confidence.

RED LIGHT, GREEN LIGHT

GOAL: Phase 3 (endurance, mental toughness, relaxation, strength) ~ Red Light, Green Light combines all aspects of breaths: strength, relaxation, timing and mindset. In Red Light, Green Light the swimmer has to control all apsects of the swim. They also have to listen and react in the water.

AGES: Two years and up

HOW: Start at one side of the pool. On Red Light, place your hands under the water in a flat position. The swimmer does a Floatie Magic. Then when you say "Green Light," they can swim. Let them know they can take a breath anytime they need it (even on Red Light). I time out my "Red Lights" to match their breath pattern. Usually I'll call "Red Light" right after they pop up for a breath.

MERMAID TIP: Praise

Dish praise according to student and their temperament. For kids under two-years-old, give praise out freely. For older children, dish out praise like a delicious cheesecake (small, but delicious bursts when they achieve new and hard tasks). For example, if your child has conquered Spin, Spin, Spin, every time they do it, don't clap with the same enthusiasm you did the first time they did it. A good thing to do is ask them, "Did you do it?" Let them say "Yes! I did it." **Give them room to take pride and ownership in what they have accomplished.**

PHASE 3: 8 KEY REVIEW ITEMS

You will need to re-introduce these exercises every time you take your child swimming.

1) Start with a small one-second submersion using Child Control Hold or Teacher Control Hold.

2) Extend the submersions to 2, 3, 4 and then 5 seconds. Let their lungs warm up and "expand." Make sure they feel relaxed under the water for at least five seconds before doing floats and glides.

3) Baby glides and then big glides

4) Floatie Magics

5) Swim Circles

6) Floatie Pops

7) My Turn, Your Turn

8) Red Light, Green Light

CHAPTER 9:
The Push Through

After your child is past phase three, there's a bonus phase called The Push Through. The Push Through focuses on mental toughness and has preparatory exercises on how to train your little one's mind to overcome panic and problem solve.

Your child will probably have a scary experience at some point in their lives while swimming. While at pool parties, I've seen kids get kicked in the face, trapped under inner tubes, and pushed in when they aren't expecting it. You want your little one to know how to handle these situations without giving up or panicking. Everything up to this point has been to set the swimmer up for success. Now that they can swim with breaths, it's time to mix it up a bit.

WOBBLY GLIDE

GOAL: Push through (mental toughness)
AGE: All
HOW: Give your child a glide, but put it off kilter, so the child has to correct their body and continue swimming.

VORTEX SWIM

GOAL: Push through (mental toughness)
AGE: All
HOW: Move to the middle of the pool. Tell your child they can choose where to swim (having so many options can be un-nerving). Watch for SCOOP UP signs, but give them a chance to push through and get to

safety if you think they can. Help them if they need it, not if they want it. Teach them their greatness by giving them a chance to succeed. (While keeping them safe, of course.)

ACROSS THE OCEAN

GOAL: Push through (mental toughness)

AGE: All

HOW: Put several toys on the opposite side of the pool and go rescue each one. The first time you swim across the pool, stay close to the swimmer. As they get more confident, stay farther and farther away. Eventually, you should be able to sit at the far end of the pool and have them swim across to you.

Once they achieve The Push Through, they are onto swim techniques.

TECHNIQUE GAMES

NOTE: This book focuses on making your child pool and swim safe. Its primary focus is not proper strokes. (That said, if your child has a strong Relaxation Base the strokes will be easy to add on later.) Here are a few games you can do with your child to introduce proper stroke technique.

~ Use a die and have older kids roll to see how many times they have to do certain exercises like kicks on the steps, laps, or other skills.

~ Have a flutter kick "race" on the steps. Both of you kick as fast as you can for a certain number of seconds.

~ Kickboard: have your swimmer extend their arms out onto a kickboard. Take a cruise! Ask the swimmer where you are going... Disneyland? Africa?

~ Center of buoyancy: How do we float? If you change body position in the water, does it affect the floatation? Have the swimmer float and then make a different shape under the water.

~ Aerodynamics: If you push off the wall and glide with your legs and arms together and in a straight line, do you go further than if you spread your arms and legs?

~ Breath control: If you inhale, hold your breath and curl into a ball under water, what happens? If you inhale, hold your breath, then slowly exhale under water, what happens?

~ Ice Cream Scoops (freestyle arms): Older kids will work on adding in rotation of the upper body, younger kids will work on proper hand placement and rhythm. Spread your hand out and ask them how they are placed into the water. Option one: fingers spread apart, option two: fingers close to each other, but not touching, with fingers extended, or option three: fingers curled into a fist. (Option 2 is correct.)

~ Pizza arms (breast stroke arms) Activity: "What's on your pizza?" Work on proper placement and stroke quality for the younger kids, with the older kids work on the rhythm of breast stroke and proper body motion in the water.

~ Star, Airplane, Pencil kicks (breaststroke kicks): The star position is feet in and together with knees bent to the side. Airplane is legs out and extended to the side, and pencil is legs together behind them. Have them practice this on the wall and also on kickboards. Once they have the positions mastered, move onto the rhythm of the stroke. The legs go into star slowly, then extend to the side, and, finally, whip fast together. After their legs come together, they should hold the position for a moment before bringing their feet into Star again.

~ Dolphin kicks activity: "Swim under the tunnel" with feet together they swim under your legs like a dolphin.

~ For any who are ready, you can add on the arms to butterfly stroke.
~ Back floats (survival and fun!): Do Red Light, Green Light with back float position being the Red Light.

POOL SAFETY

~ "Reach or throw, don't go!" American Red Cross teaches this phrase[31] and I think it's a great one! Show your swimmer how to identify someone who is in trouble. Teach them to call for help, then throw in a floatation device. (Remind them not to physically try to save another child themselves, because when a swimmer is panicked they could easily pull them both underwater.)

~ Jumping safety/diving safely: Take the swimmer on a "tour" of the pool. Where is it okay to dive? According to the American Red Cross the only safe depth for diving is over nine feet deep. Be diligent in explaining why it's dangerous to dive at shallow depths.

~ Swim etiquette at parties and get-togethers: What to do if a panicked swimmer grabs you and you can't get out? How do you handle getting stuck under an intertube/floatation device? Instead of struggling with the panicked swimmer, if someone grabs you, swim down and away from the swimmer. Swim down because the swimmer is trying to stay above the water, so if they feel like you are going down, they will usually let go. Once they let go, you can swim away. The same action applies if an intertube is over your head. If you can't get up for a breath, try to push it away, then swim down and out.

CHAPTER 10:
Swim review, must-do's & vacation tips

Your child grows both mentally and physically at an extremely high rate. I've seen swimmers be able to swim one lesson and come back the next lesson after a growth spurt and suddenly be fearful. If it's been a few months, or even a few weeks, since your swimmer has been in the pool, it's normal for them to have "forgotten." The good news is they haven't! It's all still in them; they are just out of shape. Their lungs haven't gotten a proper swim workout since the last time they were in the pool. If this happens, don't worry, just start slowly and re-build their confidence. Use the list of review items every time you get in the pool with your child.

SWIM REVIEW: THE "MUST-DO'S"!

No matter what the level of your child is, start at the basics every time you get in the pool.

Swimmers working on phase 1 and 2, the 3 MUST-DO's.

1) Breath Expansions: Start with small one-second submersions using Child Control Hold or Teacher Control Hold. Extend the submersions to two, three, four and then five seconds. Let their lungs warm up and "expand." Make sure they feel relaxed under the water for at least five seconds before doing floats and glides.

2) Floatie Magics: For kids over two-and-a-half (or any child who can isolate their arms and legs) do Floatie Magics every time you go swimming. Floatie Magics are SO IMPORTANT. By reviewing Floatie

Magics, the swimmer remembers that the water holds them up. Start with a one or two second Floatie Magic. Then extend the length of the float.

3) Once the swimmer is nice and relaxed under the water and their muscle memory has kicked in, you can add the swimming aspects. Move into glides with kicks, then play Tag. Once they have remembered how to do those activities, have them do Spin, Spin, Spin. Chances are, if you start slowly, with good a series of Floatie Magics, all of the other skills will layer in quickly.

Swimmers on phase 3, the 5 MUST-DO's.

1) Breath expansions (see exercises for phase 1 and 2)

2) Swim Circles; Swim Circles are a great way to get your child's energy flowing, relax their bodies, and help warm up their breath muscles.

3) Glides

4) Floatie Pops, Crazy Koo-Koo Bird, and Cobra: Re-introduce each exercise to re-build the combination of strength and relaxation.

5) My Turn, Your Turn. Even if your child can swim, but it's been a while, or if they swam recently but breathing is a fairly new skill, start by taking turns with them. Have them get the first breath, then help them get the second breath.

TOUR THE POOL

Anytime you are at a new pool it's good to take a "tour" of the pool. You want to identify the stairs and the shallow and deep ends. Point out any areas that don't have a wall to grab onto. Allow your child a moment to study the pool before having them hop in.

Once in, do all the warm-ups above (according to their level) and then have them swim to the wall. Every wall is different. Some have curved edges; some have gaps where the water drains. You want to practice swimming to the wall so they know how to reach up and grab it should they need to. Note: I've seen pools with NO grab-able sides. If you're swimming in a pool without sides, and your child can't pop up for breaths yet, be sure to show them where an exit route is if they fall in.

MERMAID TIP: Baja steps and hot tubs

Sometimes Baja steps (which seem kid friendly) are the scariest for children who can't swim. If you are on a vacation at a resort with a Baja step, or if your child swims at a pool that has a Baja step, you'll need to practice with them.

The water on Baja steps is usually at a dangerous level because your child can't push up to get their face out of the water from a prone position. To get out they have to know how to get their feet under them. It's not easy, and I sometimes spend an entire lesson trying to teach kids how to recover from tipping over on a Baja step.

To teach them how to stand on the Baja step, place the toys on the step. The first several times hold their hand as they reach for a toy, so they get a feel for it. Then allow them to try on their own. They may lose their footing, and you will have to guide their body as they try to stand up. Be sure to keep your hands close, because when they come up they often catapult forward.

Hot Tubs: Children should NOT be in hot tubs because of the added heat, but it's essential to have them know how to recover if they fall into the hot tub. Ideally, find a friend who has a hot tub and is willing to turn the heat down to 90. Hot tubs can be tricky because of the sitting step. The step often blocks the swimmer from getting close enough to reach up to the side, so they become stuck in the middle. You'll want to work on having the swimmer reach up high and tuck their feet under them so they can use the step to pop up to safety.

MY KID WON'T GET OUT OF THE POOL AND I DON'T WANT TO BE IN THE WATER EVERY SECOND OF MY VACATION! WHAT SHOULD I DO?

If you are on a vacation and you don't want to be in the pool every second with your swimmer, try finding a floatie that keeps the buoyancy in the correct location: the center of the body. The tubes that have center vests attached or even the water wings with the center buoyancy strap are better than just the water wings.

If your swimmer can swim, but you want to give them something fun to play with, noodles are my pick of floatation devices. Noodles are thin, so no one gets stuck under them. They are also not attached to your swimmer, so no one becomes dependent on a noodle.

If you put your little one in a floatie, always watch your swimmer. Floaties often give everyone a false sense of security[32].

CHAPTER 11:
5 Key Personality Traits of Your Child
THE SIARE FACTORS

Much of what your little one's swim journey will entail will be dependent on their personality. There are five main factors to help identify your little one's swim personality. The "SIARE" traits are specifically targeting how your little one will react to swimming. That said, it will be helpful out of the pool also. Your little one's personality may shift, based on the task at hand, but if you can identify what is happening you are well on your way to being able to help them move through the challenges life offers.

STRONG-WILLED VS EASY-GOING

Easy going children will usually follow your lead. They want what they want, but if you give them something else, they are generally okay with that, too. They are the happy-go-lucky types who make you feel like you've got the parenting thing down.

In contrast, a strong-willed child likes to control the situation. They want to do what they want to do, when they want to do it. They are independent minded and are known for digging in their heels. Being strong-willed is also a good trait. Highly independent children are usually adventurous and proactive in their learning. Plus, they are self-motivated and don't rely on you for their internal happiness. Which leads us to the next category...

High Internal View vs High External View

High external view children look to the outside world in order to guide their reactions. High internal view children, however, rely on what's going on inside of them to guide their reactions.

If your child has a high external view, if they go under the water and don't like it, when they see you giving positive reinforcement, they often will go along with it without resistance.

If your child has a high internal view and goes under the water and doesn't like it, the child will give resistance, despite any surrounding positivity. A child with a high internal view may, however, discover they love the feeling of going under and be intrinsically motivated to keep trying.

If your child has a high external view, they may have an easier time during the initial lessons, because they will be pulling from external positive energy. High external view swimmers may, however, have to overcome a Resistance Curve (See below) when it comes to phase three, breaths.

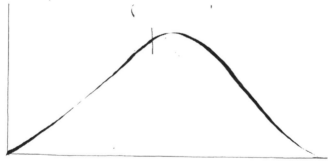

VERTICAL AXIS: Intensity of resistance
HORIZONTAL AXIS: Time elapsed or the number of attempts to overcome the task at hand.

Resistance Curve is a visual of how a child overcomes a problem. The dash is where the parent wants to pull back and give in. But if you allow the child to soar over the hump, they will discover they can conquer hard tasks. High internal view children may experience a Resistance Curve during the initial lessons where they are vocalizing their discomfort (crying) when going under the water. Once they have conquered their fear, they being to relax into the submersions.

High internal view and strong-willed children may have a more intense experience when they first get into the pool if they don't like it. They may have to work through their fears and push past their, perceived, boundaries. The positive side, however, is once they realize they can work hard and succeed, they often have an easier time overcoming fears and pushing past mental blocks when it comes to phase three, breaths, and The Push Through since they have already accomplished it during the first lessons.

RESISTANCE CURVE
OVERCOMING HURDLES, WAVE CHARTS

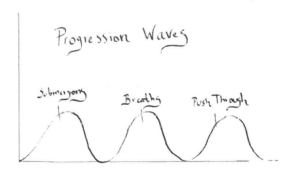

KEY FOR ALL PROGRESSION WAVE CHARTS
VERTICAL AXIS: Intensity of resistance
HORIZONTAL AXIS: Time elapsed or the number of attempts to overcome the task at hand.
Each wave represents a phase. Phase one (Floats, glides, submersions).

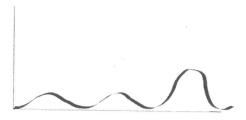

IMAGE ABOVE: Easy going, high external view.
Easy going, high external view swimmers may have a small wave
or resistance for each phase. Popping up to take breaths takes a lot
of internal motivation. Thusly, sometimes the easy going swimmers
suddenly have to face a challenge in phase three.

IMAGE ABOVE: Easy Going, high internal view.
The easy going, high internal view swimmers are usually even keeled.

They *may* have a small resistance wave for each phase.
IMAGE ABOVE: Strong-willed, high external view
The strong-willed, high external view swimmer is usually even keeled,

much like easy going, high internal view swimmer.

IMAGE ABOVE: Strong-willed, high internal view (favorable toward the water)

If a strong-willed swimmer with a high internal view likes the water, they may have a random day of resistance, but usually they are smooth

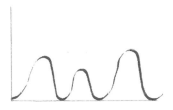

sailing and are incredibly fast learners.

IMAGE ABOVE: Strong-willed, high internal view (not favorable toward the water)

If a strong-willed, high internal view swimmer isn't a fan of the water, there's usually a resistance curve for each new phase. The plus side is, when they reach The Push Through, they are already strong, empowered swimmers. Because they have had to overcome so many hurdles, The Push Through is usually easy for them.

AMYGDALA ACTIVATED VS AMYGDALA NOT ACTIVATED

The amygdala is the panic center of the brain. It activates when we experience fear. The amygdala is our flight or fight center, and amygdala transmitters only go one way[33]. The cerebral cortex, which is the reasoning and rational part of our brain, gets instructions from the amygdala. The amygdala, however, doesn't get instructions from the cerebral cortex. How does this relate to swimming?

Let's say you're taking your child to swim lessons. You tell your child if they cry, you'll have to go away from the pool. They agree, and it seems like the best way to motivate them to not cry. But for any child whose amygdala is activated, offering logical "fixes" isn't going to help because you child's logic can't override their fear center. If, say, your child is nervous, but their amygdala isn't activated, then reasoning with the child could, potentially, work.

> **MERMAID TIP: No threats**
> Even if your child's amygdala is not activated, I wouldn't recommend threatening to leave the side of the pool. It's better to use AHM and work with them through their fear. If they need to be more emotionally firm (more on this later), then it may be best to leave the side of the pool. But it should be done in a way the child doesn't feel like they did something wrong.

The goal with Relaxation Based Swimming is to never activate the amygdala. Ideally, children learn to swim in a positive and nurturing environment. Plus, if the amygdala isn't enabled, it's much easier to explain concepts and ideas to the child. Most of the time, if the child has never had a near drowning experience or aggressive swim lessons, the amygdala will not be activated. However, from teaching the past ten years I've noticed about 10% of kids will naturally have an adverse reaction to swimming, and their amygdala will activate for no reason. All of this is okay. Knowing how to identify what is going on with your child will help you help them through it.

HOW DO I KNOW IF MY CHILD'S AMYGDALA IS ACTIVATED?

If your child is crying and screaming and it doesn't seem like they are rational or listening, their amygdala is activated. All sensible thought and manners have been shut off. Start by using AHM and Mirror and Agree. Attempt to relate to the swimmer, so they come out of their fear and join you in a place of peacefulness. Sometimes this works, if it doesn't, you have several options:

1) If your child is under eighteen months, and you're taking them to lessons, you can wait until your child is older. The crying may not have anything to do with the pool. It may be separation anxiety.

> **MERMAID TIP: Separation anxiety**
>
> Often parents are confused why their young children cry when starting lessons. Most of the time it doesn't have anything to do with the pool; it has everything to do with separation anxiety[34]. If you take the pool aspect away, and just look at leaving your child with a stranger in a new location for twenty minutes, your child would probably cry. If your child cries during the first few lessons, it's okay to continue. Chances are your child will get used to the experience after two to four lessons. As long as you are taking lessons in a place where you feel the experience is mindful and positive, learning to push through fears is a great life lesson.

2) Push through the fear. As long as your child is listening and taking good breaths before they go underwater, it's okay to guide them through their fear-sometimes, it's the only way to get them swimming! In the book, The Worry Trick, David A. Carbonell, PhD says, "If you had a dog phobia, you would re-train your amygdala by spending time with the dog. Getting afraid, and hanging out with the dog long enough for the fear to subside. Then the amygdala would make some new observations about dogs, and as you repeatedly spent time with dogs your fear reaction would subside. You can't TELL your amygdala dogs are okay. But you can create the opportunities for it to discover that.[35]"

If you have a swimmer who's strong-willed, has a high

internal view, and their amygdala is activated; if you don't push through the fear you could be on the steps for months, even years, without them ever "deciding" to want to learn how to swim. As long as the swimmer is listening, as they get used to the lessons, the fear center will relax and de-activate. If the child's amygdala is activated and you want to push through it, it's important to be the Buddha and always follow through with your activities once you tell the child what you're going to do. If you say you're going under on three, then go under on three.

MERMAID TIP: When is too old?

If your child is under two and their amygdala is activated, it's okay to wait. However, if you wait until they are five, it's going to be much harder to get them swimming. As they develop, their brains get more time to create concrete views of the world. The more time they have to form anxieties, the harder it will be to relax their fears away (this is why adults often take longer to teach how to swim than children). So don't wait too long. The ideal age to learn to swim is between two and four years old.

Self-Regulated vs not Self-Regulated

Self-regulation is shown to be one of the most critical success factors[36]. According to the Center on the Developing Child at Harvard University, "When children have opportunities to develop executive function and self-regulation skills, individuals and society experience lifelong benefits." How do children learn self-regulation? There are many ways. They learn patience by waiting in line at the amusement park. They learn to regulate their anger when they don't get the type of ice cream they want. They learn to control frustration when they can't do something they want to do. They learn self-soothing techniques by having to sit in the car seat when they don't want to or to stay in bed when they would rather run around.

The Child Mind Institute quotes clinical psychologist Dr.

Rouse as saying, "The key to learning self-regulation skills is not to avoid situations that are difficult for kids to handle, but to coach kids through them and provide a supportive framework.[37]"

Kids don't pop out of the womb being self-regulated. It's one of our biggest jobs as parents. When they are little, we "give in" to their every need (as we should!) but as a child grows, it's easier to get frustrated with crying. After all, they seem to cry at "trivial" things all the time (who cares who opens the car door?!?). For parents, it's crucial for us to remember, despite wanting our children to be happy all the time, that is not our job. Our job is to be their emotional tour guide. We are here to help them through the good times, but more importantly, guide them through the hard times. Children have so much going on in their lives (e.g. growing pains, language skills, and learning societal norms) that life can be overwhelming. Toddlers are learning a great amount every day. Self-regulation is one of those things.

If your child is strong-willed and has a high internal view, you may have the opportunity to guide your child out of their emotional turmoil on a daily basis. During each temper tantrum, use all the golden rules, but mostly AHM. Acknowledge their frustration, let them know it's okay to feel frustrated, and then help them move on.

> **MERMAID TIP: Let them overcome!**
> If your child is upset, the natural reaction is to try to distract them, or fix the problem for them. Instead of solving the problem *for* them, try to teach your child how to problem solve. For example, my three-year-old girl wanted a full can of sparkling water, "Just like mommy." I told her she could have it and then I went upstairs to shower. When I came back downstairs my toddler was crying hysterically because my husband had poured half the can of bubbly water into *his* glass. My husband had good intentions, a full can is too much for a three-year-old, but my little girl was upset. She wanted a FULL CAN of sparkling

water. Instead of giving in and getting her a new can, I used AHM and Mirror and Agree. Just by mirroring her frustrations, she immediately stopped crying. Then I asked her what we could do to solve the problem. "Let's pour it back in!" she exclaimed. "That's a good idea," I said, "but daddy already drank the water. What's another idea?" After a lively discussion, we decided to take the half full can of water, and dump it into a cup of ice so it looked like, "so much water." And, to make it even more fun, we put in some cherry juice and a straw. My little girl was so proud of herself. She worked through a problem and got something even better by the end.

Let your child discover how to move through their negative emotions and return themselves to a positive place. It's not your job to solve the problem; **it's your job to be your child's emotional tour guide.** Be an open vessel of understanding. Empathize with their plight without judgment. Often, this is the best gift you can give your child.

As your child gets older, they will have better self-regulation. Emotional maturity is one of the reasons why the swimming progression rate is faster with older children. Older children have more life experience. They know how to take deep breaths, control their emotions, and try new, and seemingly, hard tasks.

MERMAID TIP: Life lessons vs swim lessons, a case study
Little Julie is a tiny, twenty-three month old, with bright blue eyes and stringy blonde hair. By the way her parents interacted with her, I could tell she was strong-willed and had a high internal view. Her parents seemed afraid of her, as if they didn't want to do anything which would cause emotional distress for Julie because it would lead to an epic meltdown.

I got Julie into the pool and she immediately started to scream uncontrollably. Her parents watched, horrified, by the side of the pool. I asked Julie's parents if she went to classes or school. They said no, this was the first time she had any formal instruction. I told them it might work better if they watched from inside so I could help Julie discover how to calm herself down.

The parents went inside, and by using AHM, Mirror and Agreeing, Julie calmed down. (The swimmer was so passionately screaming, I was impressed she was able to overcome it.) We put the toys in the pool, and I told her we were going to do one task for each toy. Julie screamed again. She didn't want to put the toys away. (Putting the toys away is a task I knew Julie could do, but she didn't want to do it.) The majority of the first lesson was about teaching Julie how to calm herself.

After every new request, she would have a meltdown, and I would use AHM and Mirror and Agree until her emotional storm passed and she completed the task. During the first lesson, it would take us between two and three minutes between every new task to get back to a balanced state. With each lesson, the "recovery time" decreased. By lesson five it only took a few seconds for Julie to recover.

At lesson eight, Julie was still working on submersions (a relatively slow rate of progression). But what Julie was really working on during the lessons was self-regulation. Julie was learning how to follow instructions, do things she didn't want to do, and she was gaining life experiences about trust, control, and trying new things.

If you can teach your child self-regulation skills on a day to day basis, they will have an advantage when they get into lessons and situations requiring them to try new things[38].

Emotionally available vs Emotionally firm

Your child's emotional availability will change with each situation. Your child's emotional availability is a progression factor you can, somewhat, control.

Most children will be more emotionally available when their parents are around them, especially their mothers. Mothers, historically, are the milk and honey of the relationship. So children feel free to let their emotions fly when they are around. Many children are more emotionally firm when their fathers are around because fathers tend to have a little more of a "buck up and deal with it" attitude. (Of course, I've seen plenty of families where the father is the milk and honey and the mother is the "tougher" of the two.)

Most children become the most emotional firm when neither parent is present. Because the child is often more emotionally available when their parents are present, often in new situations, such as dropping them off at a new class or pre-school, it's requested the parents come and go quickly versus lingering.

Some children are more intrinsically emotionally firm than others. And most children are emotionally firm about some things but emotionally available about others. For instance, my little girl is emotionally firm when it comes to throwing up; she can vomit and then look at you with a smile as if to say, "That's better!" My son, on the other hand, is emotionally available when it comes to sickness. He'll cry and fall apart at the slightest hint of a tummy ache. When it comes to other aspects of life, for example, not getting what they want, my son is emotionally firm, and my daughter is emotionally available. Both of my kids are more emotionally firm when daddy takes them to the dentist or the doctor than when I take them.

For swimming, kids progress faster if they are emotionally firm. If the child is emotionally available, we spend more time on overcoming feelings and less time on the task at hand. Of course, learning to overcome emotions is a valuable life skill, but it does take time away from swimming skills. If your little one is emotionally available, there are a 4 tricks you can do to help.

1) The child's emotional state will change based on who brings them to the lesson. It can change if the babysitter brings them. If your child is strong-willed, has a high internal view, their amygdala is activated,

and they are not self-regulating, you can help them out by having the caregiver who provokes the most emotional firmness in them bring them to lessons.

2) If you bring your child to lessons, you can watch from inside the house or away from the pool to help your child be more emotionally firm. If you're sitting by the pool, you're like a delicious freshly baked donut they can't have. They can smell and see you but they can't have you, which will make them more passionate about getting you. If you remove the temptation (yourself), the child will often relax and become focused on the task at hand.

3) Be consistent. If you watch from inside, stay inside during the entire lesson. If you come out early or check on them midway to try to "help," the child will try to get you to repeat your behavior.

4) Keep your routine the same and matter-of-fact. If you're packing up at home to go to the pool and your child immediately begins to scream, don't shy away from what is going on. Use H2H and tell them. Then use AHM and proceed, un-emotionally, through the process. If you're strong and treat the situation casually, they will learn how to do the same.

MERMAID TIP: Parental anxiety

If you're nervous, your child will also be nervous. Going to a new class can be nerve-wracking. But remember, you're in control of your experience. If you want your child to swim, take them to lessons. As long as you're comfortable with the philosophy and style of the school, go in with confidence. If you're not sure about the school, find one you are happy with. If you want to teach them yourself, do it! There are no right answers, but whatever you decide, don't waiver. You can always switch gears, but if you go in with trepidation, your child will feel it.

4 MAIN PARENTING PERSONALITIES
(AND WHY KNOWING WHAT KIND OF PARENT YOU ARE WILL HELP YOUR CHILD.)

There are a few main types of parenting personalities I've noticed from years of interacting with parents and their children. Knowing you parenting personality type can help identify how you interact with your child.

Different parenting styles match children's personality styles in different ways. Some pairings cause frustrations for both the child and the parent. Other pairings match perfectly and both the child and the parent feel in control and at ease. Knowing your personality and your child's can help identify how to be more effective both in and out of the pool.

PERFECTIONIST PARENTING PERSONALITY

I am perfectionist parent at heart. The perfectionist parent puts a lot of pressure on themselves to make sure their child's life is perfect at all times. They rush to their side at the slightest cry. They make sure the child's schedule is perfect and the child always is where they need to be to make sure their schedule is maintained. Perfectionist parents go out of their way to explain every aspect of life and get the child whatever they want in order for their child to be happy. The biggest challenge for the perfectionist parent is to realize their greatest job is to be the child's emotional tour guide through unhappy moments, instead of trying to create environments where the child never has any unhappy moments. Everyone experiences frustrations, heartbreak, and sadness. It's your job to teach your child how to traverse "negative" feelings, problem solve, and create inner happiness.

> **MERMAID TIP: Happy is happy...**
> We all want our children to be happy. We want them to smile and run and be carefree! If they could be peaceful every moment of their day, what a glorious life experience that would be for everyone involved. Perhaps in

some alternative universe, this is possible, but not here. It's impossible for your child to be happy every second of the day. And countless studies show it's okay for them not to be happy sometimes. In the book, "How Toddlers Thrive," Dr. Tovha P. Klein PhD says, "Kids need to experience the negative in order to be able to handle it.[39]"

Life isn't perfect. As much as we all don't want to imagine it, you child will encounter negativity as they grow up. You cannot be there every second of your child's day to defend them against a bully at school, or to tell their boss at work to stop being mean. Instead of avoiding uncomfortable aspects of life, teach your child how to embrace them and then move on. Teach them how to channel frustrations into motivation. Teach them how to accept negativity without letting it break them. Don't try to fix every discomfort or challenge. Teach your child how to interact with challenges! Be sure to use AIIM so they feel understood, but then allow them space to digest life. Give them the tools to be comfortable with being uncomfortable sometimes.

Relaxation Based swim lessons are a great way to teach children how, even if they are nervous or scared, if they stick with it they will succeed. As long as you stay calm, create a safe, positive space, it's okay for your child to work through their fears.

The Positives of Perfectionist Parenting

Perfectionists are amazing parents. They often read tons of books and are well educated. They are usually very hands on and their children get lots of life experiences by going to a variety of classes and activities.

A lot of the "success" (I define success as being in a happy, empowered parent and child relationship) of a perfectionist parent has nothing to do with the parent, but has everything to do with the child's personality. Perfectionist parents pair well with children who are easy going and have high external view. Perfectionist parents can struggle if they have a child who is strong-willed with a high internal view.

4 Easy Tips for Perfectionist Parents

1) Set healthy boundaries. As Dr. Harvey Karp mentions in his book, Happiest Toddler on The Block, limit setting is an important parental task[40]. Be sure to use THE PROMISE. Your child will thrive the more they know YOU are in charge (in a healthy, respectable way)

2) Be okay with guiding your child through emotional turmoil. It's okay if they have a temper tantrum in the grocery store. You can't control what is going on inside of them, but you CAN control how YOU react. Be the buddha, use AHM and be at peace with the occasional lack of peace.

3) Remember, it's not your job to fix everything. Often mirroring your child's emotion, without a "solve" is the best way to deal with issues. If you repeat your child's concern, and allow them to come up with a solution, they are not only learning how to deal with negativity, they are learning how to solve it!

4) Sometimes it's just okay to be sad. Remember the scene in Pixar's Inside Out where Riley's imaginary friend, Bing-Bong, is upset and Joy tries to cheer Bing-Bong up by making jokes and funny faces? Joy's attempts don't work, but when Sadness sits next to Bing-Bong, Bing-Bong feels understood and is able to pick himself up and overcome his feelings.

I would, however, encourage you not to be a helicopter parent. I am a perfectionist parent at heart. I want my children to have everything perfect to make sure they have the best life possible. Many perfectionist parents take this adage to heart and place a lot of personal responsibility and heart felt ownership of any non-perfect aspect in their children's lives. I realize part of my job is to raise an independent and self-confident child and if I am going to do so, I need to teach them how to overcome challenges.

Swimming is an amazing microcosm of life. Not only are there big struggles (going from non-swimming to swimming) but also within every lesson there are small hurdles which are great opportunities to exercise the try, fail, and achieve cycle.

MERMAID TIP: "I CANNNNNNT"

I hear "I can't" hundreds of times in my week while teaching swim lessons. The "I can't" mentality comes from many factors. Maybe they hear other kids say it, perhaps in a TV show, or maybe you say it. Even if your child doesn't hear it from you, they will, at some point, say they "can't."

Encourage your child to understand the different between "I can't" and "I don't want to" If it's a task they can do, but they don't want to do, try saying:

"If you say you can't you won't. You don't have to do it, but you do have to TRY."

Going through life saying and thinking, "I can't" is no way to achieve greatness[41]. As a parent, challenge yourself to identify what YOU say "I can't" to. For instance, if your child asks you to go into the pool and you say, "I can't." you're not speaking the truth and they know it. You are physically capable of going into the pool. You just don't want to. Setting boundaries IS okay. Try saying, "You want me to go in the pool. It looks like fun. But I'm not going to go in it right now. But I'd love to watch you do your swim lesson!"

There is no one right answer to parenting. The only right answer is when you feel at peace with child raising, whatever your parenting style is. That said, I encourage you to try to let your child grow and expand. The hardest thing is to watch your child struggle, but when you take away the struggle you take away the opportunity for your child to feel frustration, work through it, and succeed.

MIXED PARENTING PERSONALITY

This type of parent is the type of parent who *says* they are okay letting their child struggle and try new things, but really, they aren't. They are the ones who sit by the pool with micro expressions cringing at every new task. They feel it's their job to fix things and make sure their child never has discomfort, but they also don't want to seem like a helicopter parent.

If you feel this, then just own that you are a perfectionist parent! If you say you are okay with letting your child work through things, but you really aren't, you're doing your child a disservice by telling them one thing and having your actions and emotions show another. Be consistent and honest. Your child knows when there's a disconnect.

As I mentioned, I'm a perfectionist parent at heart. My son is an easy-going, high external view personality type – so it was easy to be a perfectionist parent with him. My second child, however, is strong willed with a high internal view (and her amygdala activates at the drop of a hat). It's been a great life challenge to accept my role as an emotional tour guide for her.

If you're a perfectionist parent, it's okay. If you can identify and own it, you won't fall into the category of being a "mixed" type. The mixed parenting types are the hardest for everyone involved, because the truth is buried under a false narrative and the result is confusing for your child.

EXTREME PARENTING PERSONALITY

There are three kinds of extreme parents: extremely laid back, extremely distracted or extremely intense. The extremely easy going parents are great in some ways. Their child gets independence and lots of freedom to try and fail. They traverse the world and gain experiences from their failures. The challenge with this type of parenting is that there can be a lack of boundaries. The child often gets their way and it creates an imbalance of power. Sure, children love to be in control, but they also need to know that they, ultimately, have someone to guide them. Extremely easy going parents sometimes don't acknowledge their children's feelings in a way where the child feels understood. Perhaps the child becomes upset and the parents give a routine, "You're okay, honey. It's not a big deal." The child may feel isolated and misunderstood.

The second type is extremely distracted parents. I won't focus too much on this type of parenting because chances are, if you're reading this book, you are not a distracted parent.

The last type of extreme parenting is extremely intense parents. These parents seem to push their intentions for the child on to them in overwhelming ways. If the child's desires align with the parent's desires, intense parenting can yield amazing results like both parent and child are up at five in the morning to go to swim team competitions with extreme excitement!

The challenges with extremely intense parenting is if the child's interests and personality don't line up with the parent's. For example, if the parent desires the child to "man up" and swim "like a big boy", but the child scared, the result can be the parent becomes upset and the child may feel they are "bad."

When I get a parent who is extreme, I encourage them to meet the child in the middle. It's okay to want your child to "man up" and "act like a big boy," but by saying this when they are scared only makes them feel bad about being afraid. Instead, try to acknowledge their fear. Use AHM and empowerment phrases. Give the fear a hug! It's okay to be scared! Once that's established, teach them how to work through fear. I tell children they are "strong and brave" and, by me believing they are strong and brave, the child believes it themselves.

"Game" Personality Parenting

Ideally, once you know what type of parent you are, you want to strive to become a "game" parent. One who wants what's best for your child, but is also well adjusted to the idea you are an emotional guide, not the maker of emotions. As much as we all want to be there for the laughing, smiling, happy moments, your child can deal with those emotions just fine themselves. The times they really need you are the times when they are not in a happy place.

Swim lessons are a great way to let your child know it's okay to be uncomfortable, it's okay to try new things, and it's okay to fail. It's how we learn and it's how we achieve greatness.

Game parents are those who are emotionally empathetic, but not sympathetic. They embrace both the highs and lows. I would now call myself a "Game" parent. (I started as a Perfectionist parent, but through self-reflection and discovery, I have become a Game parent.)

Here are a few case studies to manifest the different parenting types. (NOTE: Names and salient characteristics of the parents and swimmers have been changed to protect the anonymity of my clients.)

Case Studies:

Case study 1: Perfectionist Parenting Personality

Sally wrote me a long email, describing her child's swim history and nap schedule, but basically, she was asking if she could come into the lesson with me. Of course, I told her. These are her lessons. She can choose the path we take.

When Sally showed up she laughed a nervous "hello." I could tell she was trying hard to be confident, but she was terrified.

Sally asked her 18 month old, Eva, if she wanted to get into the pool. The child shook her head and ran away. Sally chased her down and tentatively stepped onto the first step. When she came close enough so I could connect with her, I used a version of blanketing with Sally. I told Sally we weren't going to do anything that made her uncomfortable. If all she wanted to do was sway Eva back and forth in the water, then that's all we would do. I told her there were no right answers to how quickly we progress, but the most important thing was for her to be comfortable.

After about ten minutes of placing toys on the steps, doing Baby Glides, and Moonwalks, Sally started to relax. I could see her shoulders drop and her face muscles ease. She looked at me as if to say, "What's next?"

I told her we could have Eva do a tiny submersion. I encouraged her not to do it if she was not excited about the opportunity for Eva to learn how to hold her breath (it should be exciting!). Sally hesitated. I asked what Sally was afraid of. She mentioned "Dry Drowning" (see chapter 13). I explained to Sally what it is, and why it's rare. I also gave her signs and symptoms should they ever occur.

MERMAID TIP: Where fear comes from
Fear often comes from what we do not understand. Once you educate yourself about a topic like non-fatal drowning, you become less afraid of it.

I asked Sally if she would feel more comfortable if I did the submersion with Eva. Sally nodded. I explained to her the most important thing, when doing a submersion, is to have a positive expression. Not fake positive expression, but a grounded, calm, and serene expression of total confidence. Submersions are hard for parents because they are unsure of the process. Thusly, they aren't sure their child can do it. Sally asked me to do the submersion. I told her the child would look to her directly after she comes up from the water to read her reaction. I asked Sally, even if Eva coughed or cried a moment, to maintain a peaceful, positive demeanor.

Sally nodded, and I did a small submersion with Eva. Eva looked to me, and then to Sally, then she rubbed her eyes and let out a tiny moan of disapproval. Sally stayed calm and positive. I used AHM and Eva was fine. She went under the water like a champ. Sally was surprised, "It's like they just know how to do it!" she exclaimed. "Exactly," I told her.

The second lesson Eva didn't want to come to me in the water (she knew I was the one who does submersions!). I told Sally she had two choices, she could either not give Eva to me and we wouldn't work on submersions, or she could tell Eva what was going to happen and allow me to do a submersion. I reminded Sally there was no judgment, no right answer, only what she felt was best. The most important thing was for Sally to decide what she wanted to do. She could either not do submersions, or she could have Eva work on submersions, despite it being new and a little uncomfortable. If Sally waivered and was not confident when she handed Eva to me to do the submersion, Eva would pick up on it. Children know when you're set on following through and they can feel the vibrations of uncertainty. Sally chose to let me do a submersion with Eva. Eva fussed momentarily, but she calmed when she read her mother's calm, confident, expression. Soon Eva came to me without fussing. She knew what was going to happen, she knew she was safe, and she started to enjoy going under the water.

By the third lesson, Sally was ready to do a submersion with Eva. The first time she tried, Sally asked her child, "We are going in on three, is that okay?" I stopped her. "It's better," I told Sally, "to not give questions unless it is truly a question. Our bodies are not wired to try hard, new things. It takes bravery and tenacity. If the child is given a question, they are prone to answer, "No!" Because you asked the question, you have to respect the answer. Let's start again." "Just tell Eva, "we're going under on three," and then do it." Sally did, and Eva did the submersion perfectly. Soon Sally and Eva were doing submersions off the step and enjoying a connection in the water.

At the end of the lesson, Sally told me she was telling her husband about the swim lessons and her husband asked her how they got Eva to go under water. Sally told him, "We just have her go under!" The husband was baffled. "Why didn't we just do that before?" he mused.

The reason they didn't do it before was they didn't have confidence in what they were doing. They didn't have the understanding on how to hold their child in the water and how to properly do a submersion. They also harbored fears about the water, and different terms the media likes to throw around to make parents fearful.

By the end of the eight lesson session, Eva was loving every second of swimming! She was gliding and diving to the bottom. Sally was thrilled, and so was Eva. In eight days, both mother and daughter had overcome fears and gained new life skills.

CASE STUDY 2: MIXED PARENTING

Angela had short, blonde hair and her child, Brady was 20 months and had even shorter blonde hair. Brady was tall for his age, highly independent, and had a high internal view.

The lesson was a mommy and me lesson. Once in the pool, Angela immediately told me she didn't want the child to do anything the child didn't want to do. If a child is easy going with a high external view, sometimes this doesn't create a road block. Angela's child, however was strong willed with a high internal view. He was also low self-regulating, emotionally available and his amygdala was easily activated. Brady had no interest in going under the water or, for that matter, even near the pool.

If Angela was a perfectionist parent, it would have been easier to transition the child into the lessons. If Angela truly didn't want Brady to do anything Brady didn't want to do, it would be a non-issue. But Angela clearly wanted Brady to swim and follow along with the lesson.

In order to ease Angela's frustration, I told her just having fun with Brady in the water was more beneficial than an emotional tugging between her wanting Brady to do something, but Brady not wanting to do it. I explained it would be better to take all the pressure off the lesson if she wasn't going to "force" Brady to try new things. During the first lesson, Angela spent the entire time with Brady clutching her.

On the second day, Brady's nanny, Ericka, came to the lesson. Ericka wasn't nervous about the water. She used to teach swimming when she was younger and was excited to see what Brady could do. To my surprise, Brady not only dipped his toes in, he was amazing under the water! He could glide out from the step with perfect breath control. It was like a completely different child was at the swim lessons.

At lesson three, Angela was back with us in the lesson. Brady again refused to do anything. I encouraged Angela to be at peace with the "child led" process if she wished to go down that path. I told her just to let Brady stay on the step, and when he was ready, Brady may surprise us with wanting to swim. Angela looked concerned. Ericka had told her about the previous lesson, how Brady went under and did great. I told Angela that Brady was very capable under the water. If Angela wanted him to go under, I told her to be calm, and do a submersion with Brady. Brady was fully capable of it. I could tell Angela was torn. She wanted Brady to show her what he could do, but she also didn't want Brady to be upset.

At lesson four, Angela said she was ready to try a submersion. She told Brady they were going under on three, but when the child began to protest, Angela didn't have Brady go under. I encouraged Angela to be aware of her language. If she wasn't going to have Brady do anything he didn't want to do, that was okay. But it would be best to phrase her directions to Brady in a way trust would be established. For example, Angela could say, "Would you like to glide to me or would you like stay on the step?" Whenever a question is asked, Angela needed to be okay with the answer and follow through accordingly.

It's okay not to put your child under the water, it's okay not to teach them to swim if you decide they are too young or not ready. It's okay to not take swim lessons when your child is twenty-months-old. But what's hard on the child is when your decisions and your desires don't match.

MERMAID TIP: Is swimming necessary?

If your child didn't want to put on their seat belt, would you make them? If they wanted to run across the street without holding your hand, would you let them?

Is swimming one of those life or death things? It's the number one cause of accidental death for kids ages 1-4, even over car accidents[1]. So, yes, I would say it is. It's okay to wait until your child is older so they have more life tools in their skill set to help make learning to swim as smooth as possible, but if you have a child who is strong willed, high internal view, and has no interest in the water, then you may have to help them overcome some fears if you want them to be pool safe. You have to decide the best path for your child, but allowing your child to never learn to swim is like telling them they don't have to wear a seatbelt when they drive a car.

CASE STUDY 3: MIXED PARENTING PERSONALITY

The mom, Krista, had dark wavy hair and her son, Jackson, had matching dark locks. He was on his second immersion and could swim like a fish. He was pool safe, he could take breaths and swim the entire width of the pool easily.

At this immersion, the thing he needed was The Push Through – that added layer of protection and mental ability to push through if he got tired or scared when he was swimming.

During a swim across the pool the long way, Jackson stopped in the middle and started to call for help. I could see the mom's face morph into sheer panic. From years of experience, I could tell the child had the physical prowess of to make it the rest of the way across. What he needed was the mental toughness to overcome his momentary fear, and get to safety. I didn't want to immediately reach out, scoop him up, and take away the opportunity for him to know his own strength. He continued to wail and tread water, and I could tell the mother was getting more and more nervous, so I gave Jackson a gentle hand. Krista's face looked like she had just seen a ghost. I smiled at her and explained the theory about Jackson needing to know how to overcome panic so, should this happen when no one was looking, he wouldn't drown. She nodded, "I want him to be able to save himself" she said. I told Krista we would only work on The Push Through if she was comfortable with it. She needed to want her child to have mental toughness if the process was going to work.

All while this was going on, Jackson (four-years-old) was listening. He knew he was going to have to work through it, but he didn't want to. It was HARD! He began to protest. I told Krista we wouldn't re-visit The Push Through today, but if she's wanted to re-visit The Push Through at the next lesson, to let me know. I told her to think about it, and I told her Jackson would never be in danger. I was right there to scoop him up if he truly needed help. (If he was treading water calling for help, he didn't really **need** help yet. He just **wanted** help! If he had continued swimming he would have made it the five feet across easily instead of treading and requesting help.)

Next lesson Krista had talked to her husband and said they wanted Jackson to gain the mental toughness needed to not succumb to panic. They wanted to know he could save himself if he got scared going down a water slide or if he got trapped under an inner tube.

After a warm up, I started Jackson at the shallow end and told him we were swimming all the way to the other side. Half way across the pool, Jackson started to cry for help. What a great chance to have him understand how to overcome fear and succeed! Jackson is a strong swimmer; he could easily make it to the other side, so I knew his reaction was purely emotional. (I watch children eight to ten hours a day and I can easily spot a child who actually needs help.) Krista, on the other hand, couldn't tell the difference. All she saw was her son panicking. Krista stood and raced around the side of the house, scared to watch. When Jackson saw his mother leave in a panic, he panicked even more. I scooped him up, not because he needed help, but because I didn't want him to think he was doing something wrong by needing help. I didn't want him to associate his mother panicking and "leaving him" with him wanting help in the pool.

Krista came back around from the side of the house, and she apologized for running away, but Jackson could tell his mother was frazzled. He felt that she didn't think he could do it. If the parent is scared for their child, then the child will be scared.

The next lesson, Jackson worked himself up about the entire event. Krista decided not to have Jackson work on The Push Through. I could tell Krista was nervous to tell me, but I loved that she embraced a decision she felt good about. Again, there's no right answer. The only time the strategies are going to work is if everyone is on the same page. When parents' have mixed emotions, saying they want one thing but not actually wanting it, that's when things get complicated. Krista owned up to the fact she didn't want to watch him struggle. She saw Jackson as potentially failing, whereas I saw him as having an ability to overcome something hard and succeed. But until both of us see the experience the same way, no one will be comfortable.

CASE STUDY 4: EXTREME PARENTING PERSONALITY INTENSE

A tiny three-year-old, Sam, with large tearful eyes came near the pool. He was nervous and crying. His parents, Hal and Jennie, told him to, "Be a big boy and stop crying." Sam cried harder.

I asked Hal and Jennie if they were comfortable if I picked Sam up and brought him into the pool. They agreed. Sam clung to me, scared to death. His body quivered. His parents told him to, "Stop being so silly." Sam continued to wail. Hal and Jennie were trying to be good parents; they wanted him to do the lesson properly, they expected him to be able to listen and learn. Sam, however, had a different swim journey in mind.

Jennie offered to give Sam a lollipop if he stopped crying. Sam stopped crying momentarily, but it only lasted two seconds (his amygdala was activated, and a lollipop wasn't going to fix it).

Jennie and Hal looked to me, wondering what to do. I asked them if they would be comfortable watching from inside. They agreed, and to their credit, they stayed inside during the duration of the lesson. By keeping the environment consistent, Sam had the advantage of being able to focus on the task at hand.

I looked Sam in the eyes, placed my hand on his chest and the other on his back and I told him, "You're scared. It's okay to be scared. It's okay to cry." Sam's eyes widened as if it was the first time anyone ever accepted him in moments of peril. I repeated, "It's okay to be scared. It's okay to cry." Sam's chest stopped heaving. He looked at me with relief and curiosity. I continued, "I'm here to keep you safe, I promise."

Sam calmed down. He felt understood because his feelings were accepted. During the eight lesson series Sam continued to cry on and off during each of the lessons. But he was listening and learning. And, even though he was crying every now and then, he was also achieving joy at each task he overcame. At lesson one, it was hard for him to get in the pool and go under. By lesson three, he could glide from the steps. During lesson four, he loved gliding out to me, but he didn't like gliding to the wall. By the last lesson, he was excited to swim out to me, and to the wall. And even though fear would still creep in every now and then, Sam knew he could overcome his panic.

Sam did a second eight-series a little later in the summer. By the end of the second series he was swimming across the pool the long way taking breaths. He would still cry at the introduction of every new task, but he would get intense joy when he accomplished it.

PERSONALITY PAIRINGS AND COMBINATIONS:

CHILD PERSONALITY: EASY-GO-LUCKY

Easy going, high external view, amygdala not activated
(emotionally firm OR available, self-regulated OR not)

Lesson progression: This type of child will learn quickly and seemingly easily using the Relaxation Based Method. They will enjoy the process and the lessons will be smooth and calm. Sometimes the swimmer will experience a road bump when they reach phase three, breaths. Breaths are hard and they need enough courage to push themselves up and out of the water to take a breath. An Easy-Go-Lucky personality type may also have more to overcome in The Push Through phase.

Easy-Go-Lucky pairs well with: Game and Perfectionist parenting. A child who looks to their parents to see what will make them happy will usually go with the flow. This will create a happy parent, and (thusly) a happy child!

Easy-Go-Lucky clashes with: Extreme parenting. The type of child who seeks external reinforcement from their parent can feel lonely if the extreme parent is extremely easy going or extremely distracted. They can feel like the parent isn't paying attention or giving them the praise they crave. On the flip side, the extremely intense parent can be too much for this child. They may shut down and then feel "bad" when the extreme parent tells them to "be a big kid and stop crying."

Easy-go-Lucky is neutral with: Mixed parenting.

CHILD PERSONALITY: SATURATED

Strong willed and high internal view.
(The child is even more saturated if they have: amygdala activated, if they are not self-regulated and if they are emotionally available.)

Lesson progression: If the child is strong willed and internally motivated to swim, this type of lesson can be incredibly powerful. If they like the water, the swimmer will be resilient and power through physical and mental tasks. They will progress quickly and love the challenges the water brings!

If the child is strong-willed and internally motivated NOT to go in the pool, the lesson can be tough for the parents during the beginning stages. There can be tears, but there is a silver lining; because the child's reaction is so viscerally "negative" toward the water, they, eventually, love it even more. Once they learn to calm their bodies and emotions, their internal joy at overcoming each task will be palpable. Once they understand the water, they will be self-motivated and thrive! They will also already have The Push Through mastered, since they had to overcome it in the first phases of swimming instead of at the end.

If a child doesn't have the capacity to self regulate yet (children under eighteen months - two years) the lessons can be slower, progression wise, because the child is still learning self regulation.

If you have a saturated child, you may want to wait until they get the self regulation part of their equation in play before teaching them to swim. It will make for a shorter, less intense process. That said, if you have the time and resources, the earlier your child learns to swim, the sooner they will gain life saving skills. And remember not to wait too long!

Saturated personality pairs well with: Game parenting. Game parents can go with the flow for these mercurial personalities. Game parents know how to be the Buddha, they understand their job is to help their spirited child navigate through his/her experiences.

Saturated personality clashes with: Perfectionist parenting and mixed parenting. These two parenting types often feel helpless and out of control when dealing with a saturated child. The child will pick up on parenting boundaries not made of solid stone. They will find the weak part of the boundary and, with their tenacity, figure out a way to get through it! The strong-willed nature is a brilliant attribute later in life, but when your toddler is being stubborn about what shoes to wear, it can be taxing! Saturated kids also tend to be very emotional, and it can be hard for a perfectionist parent to not feel responsible for their child's tantrums.

Saturated personality is neutral with: Extreme parenting. If the parent is extremely distracted, a child who has high internal view may not even notice. They will be happy to move through life to the beat of their own drum! That said, the road block can be when the child has a melt down or needs emotional empathy.

If the parent is extremely easy going, the child will have the freedom to roam and the parent won't mind the emotional turbulence accompanied by the frenzied life of a toddler. The road block for an easy going parent is to still give the child boundaries so the child learns how to self regulate.

If the parent is extremely intense, as long as the child's personality and the parent's personality meet, they will be able to co-exist. The parent will put up firm boundaries, and the child will feel secure in knowing they are taken care of. The road block is to make sure the child doesn't feel shame for their "less acceptable" emotions.

CHILD PERSONALITY: TENTATIVE
Easy going, high external view
(amygdala activated, not self regulated, and emotionally available)

Lesson progression: This type of child is usually easy going, but they may have had a bad water experience in the past. Or perhaps, they just don't like water on their face, or maybe they don't trust the water or swim instructors' due to being pushed too far too fast by an instructor who uses the "drag and pull" method. (See below)

Tentative personality type lessons are usually smooth with Relaxation Based Method. The key for the tentative personality type is for them to feel SAFE and respected. Once they know what to expect during the lessons and they establish trust with the instructor they will progress very well.

Tentative personality pairs well with: Game and Perfectionist parenting. Lessons go well if the child is taken to a Relaxation Based swim class for both these types of parents. (Tentative personality will not pair well with a swim class that is less in tune with the child's emotions.)

Tentative personality clashes with: Extreme parenting and mixed parenting.

> ### MERMAID TIP: Drag and pull method
> The "drag and pull" method is where the instructor grabs your child's arms and pulls them through the water until your child is okay with it. Some children (usually the easy-go-lucky, who are emotionally firm and their amygdala isn't activated OR the strong willed, high inward view who are excited to swim) can learn this way. With the "drag and pull" method the instructor is relying on the undertow of the water to pull the child out and make it look like they are "swimming." It's okay to use the undertow, initially, to allow the child to feel movement in the pool. But be sure your child can, eventually, swim without relying on the undertow. A good test to see if you child can actually swim is to place them at a stationary position and see if they can propel from point A to B without any assistance.

CHILD'S PERSONALITY: EXCITED

Easy going, high internal view
(amygdala not activated, self-regulated, emotionally firm OR available)

Lesson progression: The excited child will jump in without a care in the world! Not able to swim, who cares? They go for it anyway! Since the child is often caught up in their own mind, its more effective to do lessons where I am physically moving their body in a way where they naturally learn how to swim. These lessons have very little talking. They are all about having the child feel how they move in the water, and what happens if they move different ways. These children are ready to go and need their bodies to be molded and shifted so they learn "on their own."

Excited personality pairs well with: just about all parenting styles! (Even mixed parenting because the child is unaware of the parents' trepidation.) They are just going to do what they are going to do, so look out world!

CHAPTER 12: Case Studies

No two children are exactly alike. As you teach them how to swim, you'll be trying different techniques to see what matches their learning style. By reading the following case studies, you'll gain insight into various swim journeys. The case studies are organized from oldest to youngest! (NOTE: Names and salient characteristics of the swimmers have been changed to protect the anonymity of my clients.)

> **MERMAID TIP: Read the mermaid tips**
> If you want to gather tips and insights, without reading every case study, just read the Bubbles for Thoughts in this chapter. They cover a range of topics and will give you kernels of juicy information to take with you both in and out of the pool.

CASE STUDY 1: PATRIK

Child Personality: Easy-Go-Lucky (Easy going, external/internal mix, amygdala not activated, self-regulated, emotionally firm.)

Parenting Personality: Game

Age: 4 years

Lesson 1: Phase 1

Patrik had been taking swim lessons from a different instructor/school since he was ten months old. When he came to my class, the mom said, "It's a personality thing. The lessons just aren't taking." I began the first lesson and could see the challenge for Patrik was he had never been taught with a Relaxation Base. He didn't know the water would hold him up. We focused on Floatie Magics and his swimming immediately improved.

Lesson 2: Phase 2

We started with Floatie Magics, and once he could float on his tummy for five seconds, we moved on to glides without kicks or arms. Since Patrick is four, he understands these concepts and mastered glides within minutes. Now that he was nice and relaxed in the water, I told him to add kicks. Suddenly, he was swimming like a fish.

Lesson 3: Phase 2 part B

We started with floats and glides, then we added arms and legs, and then we moved into phase 2 part B (swimming with intention exercises).

Lesson 4: Pahse 2 part B

We continued with swimming with intention and then added jumps from the wall. Patrik is now pool safe (he can jump in, turn, and swim to the wall). Then we moved on to phase three.

Lesson 5: Phase 3

The first day we did breaths Patrik said his belly hurt.

MERMAID TIP: My belly hurts

When learning how to take breaths, the feeling of a belly ache can happen for several reasons: one is drinking too much water (but I'm meticulous to make sure their breath control is locked in BEFORE we add breaths on, so this isn't the case for Patrik). The more usual culprit is a feeling of fatigue in the diaphragm. It's hard to control your breath, and for most kids, this is the first time they are thinking about it. Popping up for breaths gives the diaphragm and lungs a workout[42]. Another reason for a belly ache could be because they are swallowing some air during the pop up[43]. If your child has a lot of gas or burps after swimming, this is probably what is happening. It will even out once the child's breaths become more practiced.

Lesson 6, 7 and 8: Phase 3

By the 8th lesson, Patrik could swim across the whole pool with breaths.

CASE STUDY 2: JACOB

Child Personality: Saturated (Strong willed, internal view, amygdala activated, low self-regulating, emotional available)

Parenting Personality: Mom = extreme, easy going. Dad = Game

Age: 3.5

LESSON 1: PHASE 1

We started the lesson with Jacob screaming and running away from the pool like it was the worst thing he had ever seen. The mom, Stephanie, was bewildered and looked at me helplessly. I recommended she go to him and let him know he was going to do a swim lesson and it would be great.

I could tell Jacob was very independent-minded and Stefanie created a space where he was the leader 99% of the time. Stephanie wasn't having any luck wrangling him as he raced around the yard screaming. I asked Stephanie if she was comfortable if I went to get her son. She said, "Sure."

I approached Jacob slowly. He froze. I knelt at his level. I put my hands on his shoulders and locked his gaze. I said, "I'm Michelle. I'm here to teach you how to swim. I will keep you safe, I promise. I'll always tell you what we are going to do and we will do it together." I paused, and let this sink in. And then I said, "Would you like to go to the pool yourself, or should I carry you?" Jacob didn't move, so I scooped him up and took him to the pool. He began to scream again. I waited until we were in the water and then I held him close and said,

"You want to get out. You don't want to go swimming. You want to get out." He looked at me, stunned I could read his mind. Then, he started crying again. I repeated myself and added, "I'll help you get out, we just need to put the toys away, play the dolphin game and then we can get out."

When Jacob calmed down, I moved to the steps. Jacob clung to my fingers. I could tell Jacob had never stood in the water before. I said, "I've got you. Let's just stand here together for five seconds." And I held him around his chest as he stood, shaking. Then I scooped him up and hugged him and said we were going to try it again. I set him back on the steps. We did this a few times with my grasp becoming lighter and lighter on his stomach and back until he could stand on the step without clutching me.

Then we moved to the toys. We threw each toy into the pool, and I clapped after each one. "See! You can do this!" and then I picked up one toy and asked the toy, "What do you want to see?" and the toy wanted to see a Moonwalk. Jacob began to cry again. I used H2H and empowerment phrases and told him I would keep him safe. I held his hands as we walked from one side of the step to the other.

After a few Moonwalks, I had Jacob do a baby glide. I told him we were NOT going under the water. I used the first hold. I reminded Jacob to keep his hands out, like Superman.

I could tell Stephanie was nervous, so we didn't do submersions the first lesson. Instead, I showed the toys how to go under on the count of three, so Jacob could start thinking about the concept for the next lesson.

Lesson 2: Phase 1

Jacob began the class by screaming and chucking the toys into the middle of the pool. I didn't react, I simply brought him out with me as I picked up the toys with my feet. I asked him to throw the toys on the step. It took a few tries, but once he figured out I wasn't going to give up, he did.

We did a few Baby Glides and then moved into submersions. When I told him we were going under on three, he resisted, but I was already counting, and he did a great job, despite a few tears.

MERMAID TIP: Empowerment phrases vs "negative" labeling

When I first developed Relaxation Based Swim, I would train my instructors never to use "fear" based words. The reason is, often times, parents place their emotions on the child. I hear lots of parents ask their children if they are scared when it's the *parent* who is scared. (The child would be perfectly fine if the parent didn't mention the word "scared." Suddenly, because the word "scared" is in the mix, the child thinks they must have something to be scared of!)

Ninety percent of the time this is true. I still recommend not using words which have a negative subconscious subtext. Words have power, and even just by saying a negative word it will affect the listener's subconscious[44]. That said, for a child who is strong willed, who has an internal view, and is truly scared, I recommend labelling their feeling truthfully. If you try to twist their feeling by saying something like, "Are you so excited?" when they really aren't, you break their trust. If you acknowledge their feeling in a neutral and empathetic way, and then tell them it's okay to be scared, often this is enough to move them past their fear. Being scared IS okay. You just don't want a child to be scared if they aren't already scared.

Another word I used to avoid, but have recently added to my lessons is the word, "hard." A positive spin on this word would be, "Is this a challenge?" I use that phrase a lot too, but I no longer shy away from the word "hard" in my lessons for several reasons.

First of all, two-year-olds don't quite know what "challenges" are. But, they know what "hard" is. Secondly, the word "hard" has a cultural connotation of being "bad" but it shouldn't be. The more a child can hear the word, "hard" and then accomplish the task at hand, the more the child will approach other "hard" things in life and know they can overcome them. Thirdly, the more they hear the word "hard" in a context where I'm using it in the positive (e.g. Is it hard to dive down and get the toy? Yes! It's hard! Let's try again. It's okay if you miss, you have to keep trying!) the more they will think of hard things as challenges and be more likely to tackle hard things in other aspects of their lives.

LESSON 3: PHASE 1

The father, Brad, brought Jacob this time. Jacob is more emotionally firm around his dad than his mom, because he knows his dad isn't going to give in to his every whim.

I started with small submersions with Jacob, and there were no tears! We did Floatie Magics, and Jacob did a good job keeping his arms and legs still (I didn't release him in the Floatie Magics yet. I just worked on him placing his face in the water and holding his breath). I moved back to the step to work on Baby Glides, and even got Jacob to smile as we laughed at each toy wanting the same thing (going under).

The first time we did a little release, Jacob got nervous. I used H2H and told him the water would hold him up, and I would keep him safe. By this time, Jacob had begun to trust me. We did another one second glide back to the step. We talked about how cool it was that the water holds him up. Jacob was still clutching to me on the glides from the steps, but he would release and float for one to two seconds on the way back to the stairs.

MERMAID TIP: Glides

Every child is different. Some are more relaxed gliding out to you, and others are more comfortable gliding back to the stairs. Jacob was more relaxed going back to the stairs. The primary goal is to have swimmers feel the water hold them up, so if there's fear on the way out to me, but they are relaxed going back to the stairs, then I start by only doing full glides back to the stairs until the swimmer relaxes into them.

Jacob was still closing his eyes under the water. It's a saltwater pool, which is harder on your eyes than a mildly chlorinated pool, so I didn't mind if he used goggles, but Jacob has no interest in using them. I preferred Jacob learn without goggles anyway, so I didn't push the issue. Usually, kids will open their eyes the more they get comfortable.

LESSON 4: PHASE 2

Jacob's mom brought him, and there were a few tears again. The pool salt levels felt high to me. If the levels of salt are high, it can be tough on kids' eyes. I told Jacob he had to just do three toys with the goggles on, and then we would talk about taking them off again. He tried the goggles, and as I anticipated, he liked them. During the rest of the lesson, he started to relax doing glides and floats because he could see under the water!

MERMAID TIP: Newness = Bad

Sometimes kids don't want to try things because they are new. As Donna B. Pincus, Ph.D. (Director of Child and Adolescent Fear and Anxiety Treatment Program, Center for Anxiety and Related Disorders, Boston University) says in her article *Helping Kids Get Past the Fear of Trying Something New*, "Being brave doesn't mean that a child never experiences fear. It means that she is learning to cope with a range of emotions, even the uncomfortable ones.[45]"

Telling a swimmer to try it a certain number of times and then they can stop is a good method to get them to try something new. I like to give the swimmers small, achievable steps. Soon they will realize it's not so hard!

Lesson 5: Phase 2

Jacob started out with a few tears saying he didn't want to get in. His mother looked frustrated, I asked her if I could carry him in. I did H2H and asked Jacob if he wanted to come in by himself or if he wanted me to carry him in. He didn't answer, so I carried him in, calmly and gently. Once he was in, he was great! Jacob did glides and even jumped out to me on his own. He was holding his breath five seconds (once a swimmer can hold their breath for five seconds I can start doing releases with them.) Jacob was a tall kid for his age, so he was having trouble coordinating his kicks, but it was not stopping him from having a good time.

Lesson 6: Phase 2

Jacob got into the pool and immediately started to do glides without any resistance. Jacob still clenched his fists sometimes, but was good at holding his breath. He didn't quite understand how to make himself propel in the water, so we worked on Spin, Spin, Spin to help him discover how to move in the pool!

Lesson 7: Phase 2 part B

Jacob came in right away, excited to try out his new skills! He was swimming, but not with intention yet. So we started practicing swimming with intention.

Lesson 8: Phase 2 part B

Jacob was swimming, but because he was large for his age and wasn't entirely coordinated in all the aspects of his body jumping in, turning, and swimming to the edge was tricky. Most three-and-a-half year olds can do the turn around jump after eight lessons, but every child is different. Jacob is now loving his new skills and will progress quickly since he's comfortable.

MERMAID TIP: Submersion Troubleshooting: Nervous breathing, eyes closed, mouth open

A) Nervous breathers: A nervous breather is when they get close to the water they begin to inhale and exhale quickly. If your child is doing this, it is hard to time the submersion. If your swimmer is a nervous breather, have them work on bubbles. (The primary intent is to extend the amount of time the swimmer can hold their breath. Bubbles also help them to isolate their breath and become aware of how to control it.) You can save a lot of lesson time by working on this in the bathtub. The more practice your little one has, the sooner they will be able to hold their breath correctly.

B) Eyes closed. If your little one is shutting their eyes underwater, keep using EP like, "Did you know you can see under the water?" "It's so cool to see under there! It's like your superpower!" You can also try, "When you open your eyes I'll be so excited!" (And then when they do, cheer!). For older kids, you can also have them guess how many fingers you are holding up under the water. But for some, it just takes time, so keep having them practice. Eventually, most will open their eyes. If it feels like you've tried for five to six lessons and it's stalling their progress, you can use goggles as a crutch. Teach them to swim with goggles on, and then be sure to practice without them on later to make sure they can swim both with and without goggles.

C) Mouth open: Many parents worry about their child opening their mouth under the water. It's okay if they are – so long as they aren't inhaling or swallowing water. I have a lot of little kids who jump in and go under with a HUGE open smile on their face. Eventually, they will close their mouth. In the meantime, demonstrate how to take a Pufferfish breath, and keep working through the exercises.

CASE STUDY 3: TAMMY

Child Personality: Easy-Go-Lucky (Easy going, high internal view, amygdala not activated, high self-regulating, emotionally firm)

Parent Personality: Game

Age: 3 years

Lesson 1: Phase 1

Tammy was very tall for her age. Sometimes, when a child is tall, it can be harder for them to isolate and control their bodies. Tammy had been taking lessons since she was a baby at another facility. She could go under water, but she thrashed and swung her arms and legs and didn't get anywhere. Sometimes the momentum would propel her through the water as she was thrashing and it would give the illusion she was swimming, but if you placed her in the water at a stationary position and told her to swim to the side, she would not be able to. During our lesson, I did a lot of Bracing and Swim Circles to help her control her body.

Lesson 2: Phase 2

Tammy is easy going with a high internal view. When this happens, the child is super easy going, but they often move to the beat of their own drum. When explain something to Tammy, she would nod and be polite, but she'd do it her way. Tammy didn't listen when I asked her to keep her arms and legs still for Floatie Magics, and thusly, her floats weren't locked in yet. Because of Tammy's personality type, I kept the lessons more Reggio based. Tammy would swim around, and I would place my hands on parts of her body to get them in the correct swim positions so she could learn "on her own." (Example: I'd brace her legs so they would stay up and she would learn to swim with them in a prone position.)

LESSON 3, PHASE 2 PART B

We focused on swimming with intention exercises.

LESSON 4, PHASE 2 PART B

Tammy could jump in, turn, and swim to the edge. She was doing great!

LESSON 4,5,6, 7 AND 8: PHASE 3

For the remainder of the immersion, we started to layer in breaths. By the 8th lesson, Tammy could swim across the pool the short way by herself.

MERMAID TIP: How do you know if your child can swim?
How do you know if your child is swimming? I hear a lot of parents saying their children can swim when they can't. If your child is placed into the middle of the pool, will they be able to turn and swim to the side? If not, they aren't swimming with intention yet!

CASE STUDY 4: ETHAN

Child Personality: Saturated (Strong willed, internal view, amygdala not activated, self-regulated, emotionally firm)

Parent Personality: Perfectionist

Age: 3 years

Lesson 1: Phase 1 and into Phase 2

Ethan had never had formal swimming instruction before, but he was already experimenting with putting his face in the water. Ethan had been practicing in his grandma's pool, so even though he didn't know how to swim, he was very good at submersions. We added on floats, glides, and even kicks the very first lesson!

> **MERMAID TIP: Lesson preparation**
> If your child can already hold their breath, you'll save lots of time and energy in lessons! Learning proper breath control can be the longest and hardest part of the process, but if your little one practices in the bathtub or discovers how to do it themselves ahead of lessons, you'll have a faster rate of progression.

Lesson 2: Phase 2 part B

We did warm-ups, then focused on the swimming with intention exercises. By the end of the lesson, Ethan could jump in, turn, and swim to the edge.

Lesson 3, 4,5,6,7, and 8: Phase 3

By lesson three, we were starting on popping up for breaths. We worked on breaths until lesson six and by lesson seven he could pop up and take breaths across the pool on his own! By lesson eight, Ethan was swimming like a fish.

> **MERMAID TIP: Saturated personality**
> Ethan is a great example of how a saturated personality, when the child likes the water, can make for incredibly fast progress. Ethan just needed me to introduce concepts, then he latched onto them and mastered them almost immediately. It only took eight lessons for Ethan to be swim safe.

CASE STUDY 5: HARMONY

Child Personality: Saturated (Strong-willed, internal view, amygdala not activated, high self-regulating, emotionally firm)

Parenting Personality: Game

Age: 2.5 years

LESSON 1: PHASE 1

Harmony hadn't had any swim lessons and didn't like going under the water. She was strong-willed, but since she had experience with self-regulation, she didn't resist as we worked through submersions. When Harmony went under the water, she would squint her eyes and rubs her face. Harmony was barely able to go under for more than a second. During the first lesson, we spent time on the lesson structure and gentle submersions. Harmony was also a bit nervous, so I used a lot of H2H and EP such as "the water holds you up," "the water is your friend," and "you are strong and brave, you can do this."

LESSON 2: PHASE 1

I continued to work on basics like the Moonwalk, Chugga-Chugga as well as Baby Glides. We did one submersion for each toy. I would ask the toy what it wanted to see and we laughed because the toy always wanted to see the same thing. Often the toy asked if we could do ten submersions, but Harmony and I agreed ten submersions were, "way too many." So we would do one instead.

LESSON 3: PHASE 1

Harmony's Baby Glides were extending to three seconds, so I started moving into hold #2. I allowed her body to have more of the water hold it up with each submersion, but I was sure to explain everything to Harmony as we went. Once she could hold her breath for five seconds, I would begin full releases.

LESSON 4: PHASE 1

Harmony was able to hold her breath for five seconds, so we began to work on Floatie Magics. I told Harmony to let go of my arms, and the water would hold her up. I am always careful to move very slowly because the goal is to allow the water to lift them up, so they feel the floatation before my hands lower off of them. It took a few tries, but once Harmony felt the float, her face lit up!

During each glide, I told her: "I'll hold you, then the water will hold you, and then I'll hold you again." I started small, with just releasing my hands for a second, and then we built into two to three second glides.

LESSON 5: PHASE 2

We started the lesson with five Floatie Magics (one for each finger. I held up my hand and pointed to each finger, "Finger, finger, finger, finger" and then in a funny voice I say "PINKY!" I do this after each time we do a Floatie Magic, the pinky finger being the last one. Kids find this funny, and it's a great way to get them to do five harder tasks).

Then we moved to longer glides. Harmony is nice and relaxed in the water. Once her glides extended to five seconds, I told her we were going to do an "experiment." I asked Harmony to do a Floatie Magic and then kick her legs to see what happened. She did and was delighted to find she moved forward. Then I said, "That's all there is to it! You just swam!" We did a few more swims to me, and then we did some back and forth to the stairs. Harmony's kicks were nice and efficient in propelling her forward.

LESSON 6: PHASE 2 PART B

We always start lessons with the warm-ups: Baby Glides into longer glides, into Floatie Magic. After our warm-ups, we played Tag and did a few longer swims to the steps. Once these tasks were accomplished, I began to have Harmony work on swimming to the wall. Then we moved onto Spin, Spin, Spin. Once she succeeded, we did U-turns from the steps.

LESSON 7: PHASE 2 PART B

We started with the warm-ups, then moved into Spin, Spin, Spin. Next, we took the spin to the wall. I started close to the wall and had Harmony spin and reach up to it. Then we went a bit farther out, and then farther still. Once she could spin and reach the wall from about a foot and half away, I added on the jump from the side of the pool. By the end of the lesson, Harmony could jump in, turn, and swim to the wall.

LESSON 8: PHASE 2 PART B AND POOL SAFETY TEST

After the usual warm-ups, we moved onto jumps from the side of the pool. Once I felt like Harmony was ready, we both got out and stood on the edge of the pool. I used H2H and said, "If you fall in the pool, you have to turn and swim back to the edge. I'm going to be out here, you jump in, turn and swim to the edge. You can do it." For the first jump, I guided Harmony's jump so she landed in the water nice and softly. I also lowered her close to the wall so she had a higher chance of successfully getting back to the wall. We did a few nice and easy jumps, and then I started allowing her full body weight to splash into the pool. This makes her sink deeper when she jumps and causes her to have to swim longer to get back to the wall. Harmony did great and passed her pool safety test.

After the pool safety test, we worked more on the swimming with intention by modifying the Dolphin Game to where she has to swim in a diagonal line and turn and bring the ring to me.

Note: My lessons are eight lessons over two weeks. Harmony joined me for two lesson series in a row, so her case study will continue.

Lesson 9: Phase 3

We started with warm ups and Spin, Spin, Spin, and did a few nice swims back and forth across the pool. I introduced Swim Circles in order to work on the timing and relaxation of her breaths. We also worked on the introduction to The Push Through by having her jump in from the step and choosing where to swim by herself.

Lesson 10: Phase 3

After warm-ups, we moved into Swim Circles. We then worked on Floatie Pops. I placed Harmony in the water and told her to push the water down to pop her head out and say, "POP!" Some kids can do that easily, and others can't. If they can, teaching breaths will be easier. If they don't have the strength, or, for most kids under two, the coordination, skip Floatie Pops and begin to massage their breaths with Swim Circles and Cobra.

When Harmony tried Floatie Pops, she got her head up a tiny bit, but didn't have the strength and coordination to do a full Floatie Pop.

Lesson 11: Phase 3

After warm-ups, I introduced Cobra to build the muscles needed for Harmony to pop her head up.

Lesson 12: Phase 3

I could tell Harmony had both the relaxation side and the physical sides of breathing locked in, so it was time to put them together. I used H2H on the step and I told her, "You are going to get the first breath. Pop up all by yourself. I'm not going to do it for you."(This is tricky, as you want them to know you're serious, but don't make this request unless you're SURE they can do it. I don't say this unless I'm 99 percent sure the child will do it.) Harmony did pop up and I cheered! Getting breaths is a huge deal, so the more positive reinforcement, the better. Once they can pop up, and the more they practice, the better they will become.

Lesson 13: Phase 3

We started with warm-ups and then moved into Swim Circles. Then we transitioned into Floatie Pops. Harmony popped up one time for each finger and said "Pop!" each time. If she didn't say pop I didn't count it. We then moved to the side of the pool and I told her we were going to take turns getting breaths. She would get the first breath all by herself and then I would help her get the second breath (My Turn, Your Turn). We did this back and forth about four to five times. When I felt like she had the hang of it I told her, "Now you get the first 2 breaths and I'll help you with the third!"

Lesson 14: Phase 3

After warm-ups and Swim Circles, we moved into Floatie Pops and My Turn, Your Turn. She would get the first breath, and I would help her get the second. Then she would get two breaths, and I would help her with the third breath. Part way through I could tell her breaths up were getting shorter and she was becoming tense. So I relaxed it down and did Swim Circles where I'm holding her the whole time. There's a balance of strength and relaxation you have to achieve to take breaths. If you see their breaths getting tight or they aren't getting a good breath, relax it down and practice the nice easy breaths using Swim Circles. Then, slowly move back into the longer swims. Be sure to use empowerment phrases as you go.

Lesson 15: Phase 3

We started with warmups and Swim Circles. Then we did extra Floatie Magics. Knowing how to swim is so much easier if you trust the water so it's always good to review Floatie Magics. Then we did My Turn, Your Turn and built it into swimming across the whole pool the short way by herself.

Lesson 16: Phase 3

We started with warmups and Swim Circles. Then we did My Turn, Your Turn. I introduced the discussion about what to do if she got tired when swimming. I told her, "If you get tired, you take a float! Let the water hold you up, and then keep swimming and get to safety." We did a few more swims. To help her take full control of the water and I asked her, "What's an animal that's slow?" And I told her to swim slowly, like the animal she picked. By the end of the lesson, she was swimming back and forth the short way with grace.

Lesson 17: The Push Through

We began with warm-ups, Swim Circles, and My Turn, Your Turn. We progressed to swimming across the short way by herself. Now that she can swim, it's time to add on endurance. So, we did an endurance swim where she swam the long way all on her own. I used H2H and said, "We are going to go all the way across. Just follow me, stay nice and slow. You can do this." In the middle, she started to look tense and scared, and I gently held her hand for one of the breaths. My face is always serene and confident as I told her to, "Keep going!"

Harmony made it to the end of the pool. We took a break on the other side and then did an endurance swim on the way back. Harmony made it back the long way all by herself!

MERMAID TIP: Deep end fear

If the child is worried about the deep end, do some floatie magics in the deep end of the pool! Ask, "Do you float on top of the water, or on the bottom?" They will say the top (or, if not, remind them they float on the top). Be sure to take it slow and easy. Hold their hands and build their confidence in the deep end. Even if they can swim in the shallow end, the deep end can look scary. Use AHM, and H2H.

HARMONY, CONTINUING AFTER A FEW WINTER MONTHS

Child Personality: Saturated (Strong willed, internal view, amygdala not activated, High self-regulating, and emotionally firm)

Parenting type: Game

Age: 3 years old

LESSON 1: REVIEW & PHASE 3

It's been a few months; Harmony knows how to swim, but, like any exercise, she is out of shape. Swimming shape is very specific because of the breath control aspect to swimming. Even if your child plays soccer, basketball, and runs track, if they aren't practicing swimming they will not be in swim shape. Their lungs, diaphragm, and intercostal muscles can only get the correct kind of work out under water.

Since it's been a few months since Harmony has gone swimming, I start slowly and work through all of the beginning phases first (even though I know she can swim. It's so important to move through each phase if there's been a lapse in their swim practice). I make sure each stage is mastered before moving on. Harmony was suddenly afraid of sinking.

> **MERMAID TIP: Fear of sinking**
>
> If a child is scared they will "fall down in the water" or sink, there are a few exercises you can do. The first is a Floatie Magic. Floatie Magics are always the best reminder the water holds them up. Once they can do a floatie magic, I tell them to try to touch my toes (I raise my leg, so it's not all the way at the bottom for the nervous swimmers). They usually look at me and say, "I can't!" to which I say, "If you say you can't you won't. You don't have to do it, but you do have to try." If they resist, I use H2H and tell them to try to touch my toes only one time. They do Floatie Magic and reach down, most of the time their butts pop up, but they aren't able to sink. Their faces light up when they discover they can't go down. I have them try a few more times. "Why can't you touch my toes?" I ask them. "Because the water holds me up!" they exclaim.

On the first lesson, Harmony's floats were tight, both because her lungs weren't in shape and also because she was a little older and more aware of her mortality.

By the end of the first lesson, we had reviewed all phase 1 and 2, and her floats were beautiful and relaxed as she remembered the water holds her up. We worked on Breath Expanding Swim Circles. Breath Expanding Swim Circles are one of the most important parts of Relaxation Based Swimming. The Breath Expansions allow the swimmers breath control to lengthen, which allows them to feel more relaxed under the water.

Lesson 2, Phase 3

Harmony's floats were improving. She was relaxing in the water, and her breaths were much better after just a day of practice. After two breaths, Harmony would grow tired, but it will just take a little more practice for her to get the endurance she had last summer.

Lesson 3,4,5 and 6: Phase 3

We worked on relaxation, breaths, and letting the water hold her up. We do a lot of Red Light, Green Light to work on body and mind coordination.

Lesson 7: The Push Through

While Harmony was doing an endurance swim, she mistimed a breath and got some water in her mouth. She panicked momentarily, but then made her way to the side of the pool.(be careful with this phase, make sure your swimmer can recover).

Lesson 8: The Push Through and Techniques

During this lesson, she mistimed a breath, but Harmony knew how to get herself to the side of the pool easily. She didn't panic, she just got to the side and recovered. It takes practice for kids to discover they can push through being unconformable and swim to safety.

CASE STUDY 6: ANTHONY

Child Personality: Excited (Easy going, high internal view, amygdala not activated, low self-regulating, emotionally available)

Parenting Personality: Mixed

Age: 22 months

LESSON 1: PHASE 1

Anthony was excited to get into the pool. He loved jumping in and thrashing his arms and legs. Anthony had no fear, but the key for Anthony was to harness his energy. He needed to understand how to move from point A to B in the water. Also, Anthony was so excited, and he would often forget to take a good breath before he jumped in.

LESSON 2: PHASE 1

The goal of today's lesson was to slow Anthony down so he could control his breath and his body. To do this, we did a lot of Bracing and Swim Circles. We focused on taking a big breath before we went under the water. Once Anthony had a grasp on how to hold his breath correctly for five seconds, we could add on releases.

LESSON 3: PHASE 2

Anthony didn't want to get in this time. He wanted to play. (Since Anthony has a high internal view, I had to repeat his want back to him several times. I matched the intensity in which he was telling me he wanted to play at about 50%. Once he understood that I understood, he calmed down and got in the pool.)

After two lessons, Anthony's submersions were great. He could hold his breath for over five seconds. He loved to try to swim, but he didn't move from point A to B in an intentional way. Anthony also liked to spin in a circle...around and around. I let him practice spinning because it's a skill I would introduce eventually anyway. Plus, as he spun, he was working on his breath control. His crazy spinning and odd arm movements must have looked strange, but as long as he was gaining skills needed to help his swimming later, it was okay if he had a creative path. To help build his brain/body connection we also did Swim Circles and Bracing. Anthony, since he's high internal view, learned best by physical cues (vs. verbal cues): because of this, the lessons didn't have much spoken instruction, but they had a lot of physical guidance.

Lesson 4: Phase 2 part B.

Anthony's mom was letting him play on the pool steps before I arrived. As I entered the yard, I saw Anthony fall over, off the step. Anthony's Mom scooped him up immediately. He was only under water for one second, and he can hold his breath for five seconds, so he didn't drink any water. Despite this, his mom's face was tight with fear. Anthony's gaze darted from his mother's face to mine and then back to his mother's face. He began to cry, based off his mother's fearful expression. I stepped into the pool with Anthony, remained calm, and did AHM. "Wow, you tipped into the pool. That made you a little scared. It's scary to tip into the pool." Anthony was still crying, so I moved to the toys and made each of one of them tip into the pool. Watching the toys bonk down into the water made Anthony laugh. It was also a great lesson on being careful on the steps. When each toy went in, we would tell the toy, "be careful, you have to step in slowly!"

> **MERMAID TIP: Scary happenings**
>
> Often children are more scared of the reactions surrounding an event, than the actual event itself. Children look to us to gauge how they should react. If something scary happens to your child in the pool, (e.g. if they fall in from the side, if they are kicked accidentally under the water, or they fall out of an inner tube) the best thing you can do is stay calm and get them to safety in a matter of fact way. Teach them how to navigate scary situations by solving the problem, not panicking. Then use the experience as a learning tool. (Note: if your child falls in the water and they can't swim it's always best to call your pediatrician. Read more on this in chapter 13.)

Anthony's swimming was excellent; he was holding his breath and moving from point A to B. Since he was swimming, we started to add on swimming with intention. We did Spin, Spin, Spin, and Tag.

Lesson 5: Phase 2 part B

Anthony had a breakthrough lesson. He did a nice, still, Floatie Magic and let the water hold him up! Since Anthony was under two-years-old, I wasn't focusing on Floatie Magics, but he discovered it. By figuring out the water could hold him up, he was able to move through the water more efficiently.

Lesson 6: Phase 2 part B

Anthony was doing great – we worked on swimming with intention by practicing Sin, Spin, Spin and swimming to the wall.

Lesson 7: Phase 2 part B

Since Anthony is an "excited" personality, he would always starts the lessons flailing his arms and legs. Because swimming is a new skill, it would still take him a few moments and warm-up exercises to remember how to control his movements.

> **MERMAID TIP: When to take a video**
> Anthony's mom always took a video at the beginning of class, but this was when Anthony was doing the warm-ups. If you want to do a video to show progression, try to take the footage about three-fourths through the lesson. That's usually when the peak of the experience occurs. The last fourth is confidence building and can also be an excellent time to take a video filled with smiles and excitement.

Lesson 8: Phase 2 part B

We started to do jumps from the side. Anthony just needed a bit more confidence to be pool safe (not swim safe yet, but pool safe). We added the introduction exercises to pave the way for him to learn how to pop up for breaths.

CASE STUDY 7: CAPRICE

Child Personality: Saturated (Strong-willed, high internal view, amygdala not activated, low self-regulating, high emotional availability)

Parenting Personality: Mixed

Age: 22 months

LESSON 1: PHASE 2 PART B

Caprice did one series of eight lessons with me the previous summer. During the first series of lessons, we worked on phase one and phase two. Caprice was a good swimmer, but she was strong willed and didn't want to do anything she didn't want to do.

Caprice's mom, Sharon, is mixed. She said she didn't mind watching her child overcome hurdles, but she did. Sharon's Easy-Go-Lucky older son took lessons from me, so he moved through the course without resistance. With Caprice, it was a different situation. Sharon knew if she sat by the pool, Caprice would never be able to focus, so she went inside for the lesson.

During last summer's set of lessons, Sharon let her older son swim with Caprice. Caprice loved swimming when her older brother was swimming with her, but didn't like to swim alone. For last year's immersion, having her older sibling in the pool with her was a Band-Aid for the situation. The end goal, to get Caprice swimming, was still accomplished, so it worked. The challenge for Caprice during this immersion was self-regulation. Caprice's older brother was in school, so he wasn't available to take the session with her.

The first lesson, I used H2H and Mirror and Agree to help Carpice calm herself.

LESSON 2: PHASE 2B/INTO PHASE 3

Sharon had the time of the lesson wrong, so we got off to a tough start, because Caprice was in the middle of a snack and watching a show. Caprice got hurried into the pool and she wasn't pleased.

> **MERMAID TIP: When to arrive at lessons**
> Ideally, you want to get to the lessons early to have enough emotional prep time with the child, so when it's their turn, they are ready! But it's also valuable not to have too much wait time before, especially for nervous swimmers, because they can get anxious.

During lesson two, Caprice worked on how to control her emotions again. These lessons were less about the water and more about Caprice gaining self-regulation skills. That said, we did still work on her swimming, and she was doing great. She was swimming and able to jump in, turn, and swim to the wall. We were ready to add on breaths.

LESSON 3: PHASE 3

It was a Saturday lesson, and Caprice didn't want to get into the pool. The ideal, especially with a saturated child, is to make every lesson structure and experience the same, regardless of their reaction to it. So, even if Caprice didn't want to get in, it would have been beneficial to say, "It's your lesson. You go into the lesson, put the toys away, and then you can get out." But everyone has to be on the same page for this to work. Since Sharon is a mixed parenting personality (she wants the child to progress, but also wants the child to have her way) and since the child is a personality type, which doesn't allow for that to happen congruently by nature, it becomes about trying to find a way to get the child to progress and make everyone comfortable at the same time.

Since it was Saturday, Sharon suggested Caprice's older brother go in the pool with Caprice. Thus, Caprice wanted to go in the pool. Again, this was only a Band-Aid, which creates a challenge because, once the big brother was back in school, the crutch wouldn't be there. However, since the end goal was to make Caprice a safe swimmer, and since her brother could help Caprice learn how to take breaths, I said, "let's do it."

MERMAID TIP: "Reggio method"

For swimming, I talk about the Reggio method as the "child led" method[45]. Relaxation Based Swimming has elements of Reggio infused throughout it. But a full Reggio method is entirely contingent on the swimmer and the swimmer's desires. The technique is very fluid where you watch the child and see where their interests are and shape the lessons entirely around their personality, wishes, and desires.

The positives of a completely Reggio method are: A strong-willed child learns in a way they and their parents are comfortable with! They get to take ownership of their discoveries and learn fluidly. The method works well with swimmers who are strong willed who are intrinsically motivated to learn.

The challenges of a completely Reggio method: For a swimmer who has no internal desire to learn how to swim, you could spend years without progress. It's not practical for any swimmer who has a strong internal view with no interest in going under water or getting in the pool.

The Reggio method would work well with Caprice since she liked swimming, but she didn't like doing what she didn't like doing. And, ultimately, my job is to get the child swim safe, not to teach them self-regulation. (Although, I think teaching self-regulation is an incredibly important life skill.) Since the goal was to get Caprice swim safe, and because she was incredibly high on the strong-willed, internal view scale, we could have spent the next six lessons working on self-regulation instead of swimming. So, overall, it was best to implement a full Reggio method with Caprice (for Caprice, it means having the older brother come in the pool during all the lessons).

LESSON 4: PHASE 3

Caprice's older brother came in with her and she did great. She got seven or eight breaths by herself (not in a row, but one here and one there). The lovely part about having a strong-willed, high internal view swimmer is, that when they decide they want to do something, they are fantastic at learning it. Popping up for breaths, for a 22-month-old, can take a full eight to ten lessons for them to have the strength, timing, and relaxation to get their faces up and out of the water. But because Caprice is so strong-willed, she was able to do it in four lessons.

LESSON 5: PHASE 3

Despite knowing how to swim and even how to take breaths, Caprice did not like practicing her breaths if she didn't want to. For lesson five, her older brother came in with her, and I let Caprice swim after him while doing lots of physical guidance (positioning her body correctly under the water so she could pop up for a breath effectively). Part way through the lesson, Sharon came out to cheer her on. Upon seeing her mother, Caprice began to cry about wanting to get out. Sharon told Caprice she had to finish her lesson and she went back inside. We finished the lesson, but Caprice didn't pop up for as many breaths as she did during lesson four. Because the lessons are Reggio based, I followed her lead, so the lesson progression fluctuated based on her mood. I also had to infuse the lessons with guidance, but not make the lessons overwhelming. It was all about leading Caprice into ideal situations so she wanted to practice new skills.

Lesson 6: Phase 3

Caprice was still working on phase three. She swam across the pool the short way without any help. Her breaths needed more practice, so we did My Turn, Your Turn (a series where I helped her get the first breath, and then had her pop up for the second breath by herself, and then I'd get the third breath by holding her hands, and then she'd get the next one).

The idea for My Turn Your Turn is to practice the relaxation side of breaths (my turn) and the physical strength of breaths (your turn). The brain and body will eventually put those two aspects together.

Lesson 7: Phase 3

Caprice popped up for a breath and got a nice clean one about 50% of the time. If she put her mind to it, she could probably do even more than that. Caprice liked to follow her older brother and hold her breath as long as possible before coming up for a breath. This was great for her lung capacity, but made it hard, while maintaining a Reggio style lesson, to have her practice her breaths. Since Caprice could hold her breath for so long, she felt no need to practice popping up.

Lesson 8: Phase 3

We did a lot of pool safety tests with Caprice. She could jump in from the side, come up for a single breath, and get to the edge.

CAPRICE THE NEXT IMMERSION:

At the first lesson, it had been a few months since our last session, Caprice got stuck vertically when trying to get a breath about half the time. She often called for help, instead of pushing through and getting to safety. After the 8 lessons of working on endurance, relaxation, and breaths, Caprice was swim safe and was keeping up with the big kids. (Note: Caprice STILL takes lessons with her older brother in the pool most of the time, but she's a great swimmer.)

CASE STUDY 8: ARROW

Child Personality: Saturated (Strong-willed, external view, her amygdala was activated last year, now it's not anymore, low self-regulating, emotionally available the first year, the next year, was mid-range)

Parenting Personality: Mixed, but trying to be Game!

AGE: 21 months

When Arrow was 16 months, she cried through two immersions (16 lessons), but she was listening and doing such a good job. Her mom kept asking if she should stop the lessons, but Arrow was doing so well, I knew the crying would go away. By the time she was eighteen months old, Arrow could jump in the pool, turn, and swim to the edge. Her mom was so happy she continued the lessons despite the tears.

The next summer, while most little ones her age are working on phase one, Arrow could already swim like a fish and just needed to learn how to pop up for breaths.

Lesson 1: Phase 3

The first lesson, Arrow and I did warm-ups and then moved onto breath work. Her breath timing looked good because she had a Relaxation Base already in place.

LESSON 2: PHASE 3

During the second lesson, we continued to do preparatory exercises for breaths.

LESSON 3: PHASE 3

The third lesson, Arrow popped up for a breath on her own the first time. What an exciting moment!

LESSON 4: PHASE 3

At lesson four, Arrow knew she would have to work hard for her breaths, and she resisted. Aarow is strong-willed, so once she decides she doesn't want to do something, she digs her heels in. Even if a swimmer loves swimming, if they are faced with a new challenge (like breaths), they will have the opportunity to overcome a new hurdle (sometimes this involves a little crying/resistance). Arrow's mom was concerned by her discomfort and pulled Arrow out of the lesson early. She told me Arrow doesn't usually cry, so she didn't want to push it! Although it is true Arrow rarely cries, when faced with new challenges, she is emotionally available. By pulling Arrow out early, getting her to take breath next lesson will be tricky. Arrow discovered that if she resists, she won't have to try hard.

MERMAID TIP: Why is my child resisting?
Children are just like us, except they, depending on their personality type, don't usually talk themselves into doing hard things. As adults, we've learned to balance the Ego, Id and Superego[46] (balancing what we want to do and what we have to do). If we don't want to do something hard, we ask ourselves if the long-term pay off will be worth the struggle. If so, we buck up and do it. Kids, sometimes, don't

have the second part of that equation. They don't have enough life experience to think into the future and rationalize that "if I learn how to pop up for breaths, and if I fall into the pool, I'll be able to save myself."

All they feel is "This is HARD! I don't want to!"

It's how you might feel right before, say, I told you to do a five-mile run. You would probably get a little bit of anticipatory anxiety. It's hard work! What if you get tired? What if you get a cramp? What if the glass of wine you drank last night makes you dehydrated? But once you turn off the mental chatter and doubt, and you accomplished the feat, you feel so good about yourself. Children are the same; it's our job to be the yin to their yang. We need to be their Ego to their Id. We need to be able to look into their futures and say, "This is good for you. Even if it's hard at the moment, you'll be so proud once you complete it." We get to be the "rational, logical" part of their brain when their emotional center wants to go running for the hills, especially when working with breaths. It takes a lot of physical and mental energy to push the water down and take a breath at the exact right time. It's also hard because they will miss time their breath and at some point get a bit of water up their nose or mouth.

It's these moments of overcoming a challenge that gives them the life lesson, "You CAN do it! Even if it's hard."

LESSON 5: PHASE 3

Arrow could do two breaths in a row. Her mom wanted her to only swim if she WANTED to, which was a challenge because popping up for breaths is hard. Thus, I made the lessons as fun as I could, and still get breaths in. The more Arrow practiced them, the sooner she would master them.

LESSON 6: PHASE 3

Arrow's breaths looked good, but she would sometimes gets stuck in the middle of the pool, and consequently, would get tired, which made her kicks drop. I gave Arrow a focus point (my hand under the water about 45 degrees below her eye line) and told her to get a toy/my hand.

By the end of lesson six, Arrow could get three breaths in a row all by herself.

LESSON 7: PHASE 3 AND THE PUSH THROUGH

Arrow's breaths clicked in, and she was able to swim across the pool the short way, taking three to five breaths all by herself. We were working on mental toughness with her, where I'd toss her (gently) into the middle without direction, and she needed to figure out which wall to go to.

LESSON 8: PHASE 3 AND THE PUSH THROUGH

Arrow could swim the long way with breaths. We did a lot of Red Light, Green Light to help her relax and be able to swim even longer distances.

CASE STUDY 9: FOSTER

Child Personality: Easy-Go-Lucky (Easy going, high external view, amygdala not activated, self-regulated, emotionally firm)

Parenting Personality: Perfectionist

Age: 20 months

LESSON 1: PHASE 1

The mom, Rachel, was early to the lesson and the child had plenty of time to get acquainted with the pool and the new situation. Foster approached the pool with a baseball cap and board shorts His mom had a brand-new baby and the Foster was in a "mommy mommy" phase. Rachel did a good job of being calm, lowering to his eye level and saying, "you're going to go in the pool with the teacher, and I trust the teacher. You'll be great." He seemed a bit nervous, but Rachel's confidence in him gave him strength.

Rachel placed Foster into my arms. I could tell he was nervous, so I used blanketing and H2H. I told him we were going into the pool and I would keep him safe. I explained we were going to put the toys away and then play the Dolphin Game. Because Foster has high external view, I used a lot of verbal guidance for the lessons. Being told what is going to happen before it happens halted Foster's apprehension.

We did Moonwalk, Baby Glides, and then moved to submersions. Foster was a bit uncomfortable going under water, but his mother did a good job sending positive energy from the side of the pool. Foster was on the edge of crying a few times, but he didn't!

Lesson 2: Phase 1

When Foster came in, he still seemed a little nervous, but using H2H and EP phrases helped him relax. We did quite a few submersions.

Foster's breath control was excellent; he could hold his breath over five seconds, so we moved onto releases. We did a Baby Glide, and the water held him up for a second. He was startled, but I used AHM and circled him back to the steps. Since I was casual and calm, Foster followed suit.

MERMAID TIP: Keep in range of the child's emotions

There's a balance between making new experiences seem exciting but not so enormous they feel like our reaction is not authentic or like they shouldn't have been able to do what they just did. There's a kind of enthusiasm and positivity which will give the swimmer peace and confidence. And there's a kind of passion so intense and "put on" it will tip the swimmer off balance. If the child is nervous and you're too over the top with praise, it can make the child feel even more overwhelmed! **Stay within the range of their emotion**. If your child is outgoing and excited, your reinforcement can match. If your child is nervous and fearful, and you try to compensate by being extra excited, you may end up making the child more apprehensive.

Lesson 3: Phase 1

Foster's dad brought him to the lesson. Having his dad there seemed to make Foster even more nervous. Perhaps the change of routine altered the "flow" in Foster's day and thusly shifted his mood. Or, perhaps Foster is more emotionally available when his dad is around. Either way, Foster did a great job, despite his additional nerves. We worked on submersions with releases. Foster was progressing well for a 20-month-old.

> **MERMAID TIP: Schedule changes**
>
> Often a change in routine can shift a child's mood. Children thrive on structure, but it's beneficial for children to learn how to adapt to different environments and learn to be flexible. A change of plans is an excellent opportunity to discuss things don't always happen the way they "should."
>
> However, when introducing an activity with many "unknowns" it can be helpful if the schedule changes are limited. If you can, have the same person bring your child to class and always do the same routine surrounding the lessons. Once they are used to the classes, they will be able to be more flexible.

LESSON 4: PHASE 1

Foster was trying to pressurize the submersions correctly. His breath control was great during the second and third lesson, but he was now struggling to pressurize the water so he didn't drink it. There is an ebb and flow to the learning process, so this isn't abnormal. I introduced bubbles to Foster to help him visualize his breathing. (The goal of teaching bubbles isn't so they blow every time they are underwater. The goal is for them to feel and have a visualization of what their breath looks like. This way they can take a breath up, and then blow bubbles down. By identifying those two, often holding their breath comes naturally.)

LESSON 5: PHASE 1

Foster didn't like going under the water for more than three seconds, so I worked on extending his breath control. We also worked on bracing and glides.

Lesson 6: Phase 1

This lesson was about pushing past the fear of letting the water hold him up. I did more releases to help him feel the water lift him as he glides out to me. With older swimmers, I break it into phases (Floatie Magics and Glides), but with the little ones, it's better to allow their bodies to feel it and become used to it through repetition. The first time we did a longer glide, Foster fussed momentarily. We kept trying, and by the end of the lesson Foster was much more comfortable. The first time kids feel the water hold them up can be an odd experience. The more they do it, the more used to it they will be! I was sure to use empowerment phrases and H2H, and if it ever felt Foster was getting overwhelmed, I switched gears to a fun activity.

> **MERMAID TIP: Two positives for every one hurdle**
> Relaxation Based lessons, ideally, are fun! A great way to keep the lessons from being overwhelming is to pair each hurdle with two positive experiences. For example: if the child doesn't want to swim to the wall, but they do it three times, then they get to do an activity they enjoy. This ebb and flow will keep your child feeling like they are successful, while continuing to improve and gain new skills.

Lesson 7: Phase 1

Foster was doing well, but he was a nervous swimmer, so I did a lot of H2H to calm his nerves. His glides were getting longer, and his breath control kept improving. We started adding on kicks.

Lesson 8: Phase 2

Foster's breath control has evened out. He did nice and easy glides, so we started on phase two, swimming! For kids under two, learning how to hold their breaths is often the hardest part of the process!

CASE STUDY 10: JAX

Child Personality: Saturated (High Strong-willed, high internal view, amygdala activated, low self-regulating, high emotionally available)

Parenting Personality: Game

Age: 18 months

LESSON 1: PHASE 0

Jax had blonde ringlets, large blue eyes and a stream of clear buggers running down his nose. He spent most of the lesson kicking and thrashing against me, pinching and screaming. At first, Jax wouldn't even stand on the step by himself. I used H2H, AHM and by the end of the lesson he would stand on the step, but he was still crying. Despite the tears, he was doing a good job listening and putting the toys on the side of the pool. Jax's tears weren't blinding him; he understood what I was saying, and he was doing the task at hand. We didn't do any glides, floats or submersions. Jax only worked on lesson structure and learning to self-regulate.

LESSON 2: PHASE 1

Jax's lesson was night and day from the first one. He knew immediately to start putting the toys on the side of the pool. He understood the structure of the lesson, but he still cried most of the time. The only time he stopped crying was to tell me about a dog he liked. When he was telling me about the dog, I mirrored his body language. (Echoing body language is a great way to connect and find common ground. It says, "I'm like you!") I told Jax I liked dogs too, and we had a lovely discussion about dogs. Now that Jax was calmer, we moved into submersions. He did a good job listening to my count and holding his breath.

Jax's mom has a great, relaxed and empathetic demeanor. (Jax is her fourth child!)

LESSON 3: PHASE 1

Jax was fired up from the moment he arrived. Part of the challenge is that Jax uses a pacifier and blanket to soothe himself out of the pool and, since he can't have it in the pool, he's trying to figure out how to handle his emotions without his lovies. (This is another reason some parents choose to wait until their child is a little older; they have more emotional firmness even without their pacifier and blankets). Jax's mom always does the same routine when she comes to lessons: she places Jax in my arms with the belief he is going to do great, she tells him she'll be back once he put the toys away, and then she goes inside.

During the lesson, I was looking to make sure Jax is listening when we go under the water. He wasn't perfect at it, and he was still crying, but he was trying.

LESSON 4: PHASE 1

Despite crying the entire lesson, Jax was progressing well. He was listening and doing submersions with gentle releases. He could glide to the wall and do Chugga-Chugga.

I told his mom I was not worried about Jax's crying, because there are so many other progression factors involved other than crying. If Jax was crying and not listening, then I would be concerned, but he was a good listener, did the lesson, and was progressing.

LESSON 5: PHASE 2

Jax was swimming! He'd come off the step and kick out to me. Since he's under two-years-old, I skipped through the Floatie Magic phase and moved right into swimming (I'll add Floatie Magic back on later, once he has the ability to control and isolate his arms and legs).

Jax would still cry, but then take a big breath and swim out to me. At the end of the lesson, Jax did a little swim to show his mom, and his mom was impressed, which made Jax so proud of himself.

LESSON 6: PHASE 2.

Jax started the lesson crying, but he still took a good breath and swam out to me. In the middle of the lesson, I took a sip of my water and said, "AHHHH" and Jax thought that was the funniest thing ever! After that moment, Jax had waves of asking for mommy, but he swam out to me with a big smile on his face and started to be empowered by the process.

LESSON 7: PHASE 2

Jax, once again, came in crying. His nanny brought him this time, and he kept asking for his nanny. I did Mirror and Agree "I want your nanny too! I want her too. Let's put the toys away, and we will get your nanny!"

I asked Jax if he could get the toys and put them away. Jax loves getting the toys, so he stopped crying and put the toy away.

Jax was swimming beautifully out to me for about six seconds, so we were in phase two part B, swimming with intention.

We did some work on turning and swimming to the wall, and then we progressed to an introduction to jumps.

LESSON 8: PHASE 2 PART B

Jax could jump in, turn, and swim back to the wall. He found the water so amazing, he'd lean back and try to float on it.

Jax could dive to the bottom of the pool to rescue toys with me assisting him on the way down. Jax is a good example of how a strong-willed child may have an intense beginning, but how they can bloom into an incredible swimmer as they grow to love it.

CASE STUDY 11: RICHARD

Child Personality: Easy-Go-Lucky (Easy going, high external view, amygdala not activated, low self-regulation and emotionally available)

Parenting Personality: Game

Age: 18 months

LESSON 1: PHASE 1

Richard had never had swimming lessons and didn't like going under the water.

On first day of class, Richard and Sarah were running late to the lesson. Sarah was calm, despite being delayed. Sarah told me that Richard had never had swimming lessons before, but they were excited to start. Sarah asked if she could sit by the pool, I said of course, as long as she felt at peace there. I told her if she got nervous or anxious she could go inside. Sarah had a very easy going and relaxed nature and sat by the side of the pool giving Richard positive reinforcement.

MERMAID TIP: Positive reinforcement

Sometimes, the most powerful kind of communication is non-verbal[47]. Watching your swimmer in a calm, confident way is excellent. If there's a lot of verbal interaction the child, especially young children, can become overwhelmed and distracted.

When Richard came into the water, he was tentative, but he followed along with the activities. The lesson had a few tears as Richard, young at 18 months, tried to overcome the wave of emotions each new activity brought up. Richard ended the lesson with a few nice submersions. Richard cried about 30 percent of the time, which is pretty low considering he was so little.

LESSON 2: PHASE 1

Richard and Sarah were early to this lesson. Richard had a chance to look around and explore the yard. The extra time gave Richard more confidence as he came into the pool. Once in, Richard cried about 70 percent of the time.

> **MERMAID TIP: My child did better the first lesson. What happened?**
>
> It's easy only to judge a lesson on how much or how little resistance (crying) there is. But there are many more accurate ways to access a child's swimming prowess. During the first lesson the child often is more emotionally firm than the second lesson (especially children under two-years-old). During the first lesson the child is in a new situation, and they are unsure what to expect. By the time the second lesson rolls around, they understand what is happening. They know they are going to have to try new, hard things. They tend to cry a bit more during the second and third lessons. Then, once they figure out how to go under the water, the resistance usually tapers off. If you're worried about your child crying, watch to see if they are *listening*. Are they taking a good breath before they go underwater? Or are they in a blind, tearful fit? If they are listening, great! The crying will drop away when they become more comfortable.

Richard was doing great listening, in spite of his crying. I would give him a count: one, two, three, under and he would hold his breath as he went under the water (so good!). Of course, like everything else in life, it's a trial and error process. Now and then Richard wouldn't time his breath correctly. He was at about 80 percent when it comes to proper breath control (he got 8 out of 10 submersions timed properly). The submersions are only about a second long, and the primary focus is learning how to take a good breath and then hold it under the water.

> **MERMAID TIP: Perfect expectations**
> When a child is learning to walk, they fall many times. In swimming, getting a little water in their mouth, or up their nose, is the equivalent of taking a tumble when learning to walk. It's a natural part of the process. Of course, you want to help them drink as little water as possible, but they are learning how to hold their breath and sometimes they will make a mistake and forget. Luckily, the body is equipped with an epiglottis. It is the epiglottis' job is to block food or water from getting into the lungs[48]. If you get water "down the wrong pipe" your epiglottis closed too late, and you'll cough to move the water back up and out of your trachea. It's the same with swimming. (For more on this, read chapter 13.)

LESSON 3: PHASE 1

Sarah was ten minutes late to Richard's lesson. She does an excellent job of staying calm even if she's running late. If she was late, tense, and upset, it only worsens an already not-ideal situation Richard wanted to play on the slide instead of coming into the pool. (He got to play on the slide yesterday! Why not today?) I used AHM and told him after we put the toys away, he could play on the slide. Once Richard knew I understood his desire, he came right over.

Richard went under quite a few times and only cried about 20 percent of the time.

LESSON 4: PHASE 1

Sarah was early, so Richard got to play on the slide before his lesson. He resisted slightly as he came into the pool. We did quite a few submersions. He didn't cry during the lesson. He's not having fun yet, but he's not crying. Richard is pretty young, so it takes a lot of practice for him to understand breath control.

LESSON 5: PHASE 1

We started on a few glides and gentle releases.

LESSON 6: PHASE 1

Richard was still working on his breath control going under the water; he was starting to glide out on his own. Richard could do Chugga-Chuggas, Moonwalk, and all the water confidence builders.

LESSON 7: PHASE 1

Sarah told me it's Richard's last class because his dad was a professional basketball player and they needed to travel to get to the game. Such a bummer to miss his last lesson.

Richard's doing such an excellent job with his submersions and glides. Next class, we would probably have started on swimming. The breath control process for Richard was 7 lessons, which is "normal" for an 18-month-old.

MERMAID TIP: What's normal?

The "normal" time for kids to walk is between the ages of nine months – 17 months[49]. Swimming is similar in that every child has a different rate of progression.

CASE STUDY 12: MAGGIE

Child Personality: Saturated (Strong-willed, high internal view, amygdala activated, low self-regulating, emotionally available)

Parenting Personality: Extreme; easy going.

AGE: 17 months

LESSON 1: PHASE 1

Maggie was very excited at the onset of the lesson, but once she got in the pool she was nervous. After using H2H she calmed down. We did a few submersions, and she only cried about 30 percent of the time.

LESSON 2: PHASE 1

Maggie knew what was going to happen this lesson and wanted no part of it! She cried almost the entire lesson. Her amygdala had taken over.

Her mom came by the pool at one point and the crying increased. I gently suggested she tell Maggie that she would come back once the toys were put away. She did, and Maggie was able to calm down. Maggie did a good job holding her breath on submersions, but there are quite a few tears. I told her mom, after the lesson, as long as Maggie is holding her breath during the submersion, it's worth keeping her in the lessons. I explained if it feels like the lessons aren't progressing, I'll tell her to wait until Maggie is a little older.

Lesson 3: Phase 1

Maggie's older sister came to the lesson and she swam first. Seeing her sister do the lesson was inspiring to Maggie. Her aunt brought her to the lesson and Maggie was more emotionally firm without her mother there.

About five minutes into the lesson Maggie was calm and listening. We began to work on submersions and she didn't cry.

Lesson 4: Phase 1

Maggie's mom dropped her off with me in the pool and went right inside. Maggie's crying stopped immediately, and we began to work on her submersions. Her mom came out a little too early, and Maggie started crying. She asked if she should go away again, but, at that point, it was better to have the lesson be cut short a few minutes, so Maggie thought she had completed the lesson vs being taken out of the pool because she was crying.

Lesson 5: Phase 1

Maggie didn't cry at all, and her breath control was getting better. We started with a few gentle releases. Once breaths are locked in, everything else is easier.

Lesson 6: Phase 1

Maggie's mom was "hiding" behind the sofa instead of going inside, and in the middle of the lesson she popped up to say something. Once Maggie knew her mom was around, she had a meltdown. Maggie kept looking over at the sofa, and even though I was able to get her focus back on swimming, she wasn't as relaxed as she was previously because she was waiting for her mom to pop out again.

LESSON 7: PHASE 1

The goal was to get Maggie to relax and have fun right from the start. I know Maggie loves Motor Boat, Motor Boat, so we started with that activity.

> **MERMAID TIP: Humor with kids**
>
> Every child has a different sense of humor. If you can tap into what they think is funny, it's great. I often watch how the parents interact with their children to make them smile and try to emulate it. If you can find a familiar "funny" with the child, it's a great way to have them relax. Sometimes it's throwing a toy into the water and saying "plunk" in a funny way. Or it might be talking about the kind of food you like and the kind of food *they* like. Any shared experience can work. For younger swimmers, a lot of the humor is physical humor vs verbal humor. They love "cause and effect" comedy. For instance, if I throw a toy in and say "boom" after it goes in the water, the child laughs. Sometimes I say "boom" right away, and sometimes I wait and say "boom" after a few seconds. The anticipation and then the pay off of me saying "boom" captures their funny bone almost every time.

LESSON 8: PHASE 1

Maggie was still working on submersions, floats, and glides. At 17 months, it's going to take her eight lessons to learn how to calm herself down and achieve proper breath control.

Maggie's dad was at this lesson. He sat by the pool with a friendly, calm energy, but he kept appearing and disappearing. It's hard when parents change locations because the child can feel like they are doing something wrong if the parent goes and something right if the parent re-appears. Luckily, Maggie has a high internal view, so she didn't seem to mind.

CASE STUDY 13: AIDEN

Child Personality: Too early to know, but seems to be easy going and a sweet little love.

Parenting Personality: Game

Age: 10 months

LESSON 1: PHASE 1

Aiden was pleased and peaceful in my arms. He fussed a moment when his nanny went inside, but soon relaxed. Aiden was very little, so we worked on Moonwalk (the very beginning stages, because Aiden can't keep his feet moving one in front of the other yet) and Baby Glides.

We did six submersions. Aiden would fuss momentarily after he went under, but rolled right through it, as he looked at me and saw my peaceful demeanor.

LESSON 2: PHASE 1

When I arrived, Aiden was already in the pool with his nanny.

> **MERMAID TIP: Swimming before or after the lesson**
> If you have a pool or you are taking your children to lessons, it's best
> to have them start at the time of the lesson. If they have already been
> in the water, even waiting in the hot tub, they are not at their most
> fresh state. You want them with the peak mental and physical presence
> for the lessons. If the child wants to stay in the pool afterwards, under
> supervision, of course, that's a good time to practice. But if you see the
> child practicing incorrect body positions or getting overly tired, have
> them come out of the pool.

Aiden loved being in the pool with his nanny, but as soon as
she left, he burst into tears. I was able to calm him a few times, but at
about the 15-minute mark, the crying escalated into the type of cry
which I could tell was unproductive. We ended the lesson at the 15
minute mark.

> **MERMAID TIP: When to stop!**
> The goal of the lessons is to end when the child is still engaged and,
> ideally, on an up-note! If the child is young and begins crying so much
> that their amygdala has taken over, then it's time to pull them out,
> re-set and try again later. At ten months old, they aren't in the mood
> sometimes, and it's better, in the long run, to stop if they are truly upset.

LESSON 3: PHASE 1

His caregiver handed over Aiden, and he cried for a moment,
but then began to enjoy the lesson. We did a Reggio based lesson
where I followed his lead. If he was interested in a ring, I did bubbles.
If he was involved in a toy, then we worked on basic submersions.

LESSON 4: PHASE 1

Aiden fussed a minute when he came into the pool, but then
he relaxed and enjoyed his lesson. We continued to work on: Chugga-

Chugga, submersions, Moonwalk, Glides, kicks, and glides. He was progressing in each activity.

Aiden loved to "chat" during the lesson. I often echoed his noises in between describing the tasks. He laughed at the toys nibbling on his fingers or when I would sway him back and forth in the water.

We began to work on glides to the steps. Aiden did it three times and had proper breath control each time.

Lesson 6: Phase 1

Aiden's lesson was fantastic! He was relaxed, focused, and enjoying himself.

Aiden could put his hands on the step and Chugga-Chugga around to the side of the step where he could touch his feet down. He was able to freely stand on the second step with his hands on the first step.

Aiden was able to hold onto the wall with both hands and "free hang" for five seconds. We started Elbow, Elbow, Belly, Knee, Knee up onto the side of the pool. He sat on the edge and then would "fall" into the water (Humpty Dumpty). We did it three times, and he held his breath each time.

We did a lot of submersions from the step. Aiden sat on the top step and would lean out to me, gliding (without assistance) for two to three seconds before I would scoop him up. We did this about ten times and he held his breath correctly each time.

Aiden has the beginning phases of gliding back to the step. He can place his hands and pull his face out of the water.

Lesson 7: Phase 1

Aiden was a little fussy. He didn't cry, but he wasn't quite as low-key/chill as the previous lesson. He was still listening and enjoying the lesson most of the time, but he had an opinion of what he wanted to do and wasn't afraid to let me know it.

Lesson 8: Phase 1 onto Phase 2

Aiden was doing great with his breath control and glides. We started to add on kicks.

CHAPTER 13:
Preventing drowning (why we should NOT use the term "Dry-Drowning") and other hot button topics:

WHAT'S THE BEST AGE TO LEARN TO SWIM?

According to the National Vital Statistic System drowning is the number one cause of accidental death for kids ages 1-4 (even over car accidents). Despite the American Academy of Pediatrics' previous rulings against teaching children to swim before the age of four, the AAP changed their stance saying, "New evidence shows that children ages one to four may be less likely to drown if they have had formal swimming instruction.[50]" NOT knowing how to swim has never saved a child. If your child fell in the pool, without the knowledge of how to move from point A to B, their chance of saving themselves is next to nothing. I have taught thousands of kids under the age of four how to swim.

So what's the best age? It depends. If your child is "high risk" (living in a house with a pool, around open bodies of water, visiting friends' houses with pools, vacationing at places with a lot of pools, etc.), and if you have the time and resources, start them as early as your pediatrician says is safe. (I started my kids at three months!)

For most children, the best time to learn is from ages two to four. Once your child turns five or six, there is more of a transition to "adulthood" making learning to swim more challenging for them. Their cognitive development is good for your sanity, but as far as swimming goes, the fears and preconceived notions can be harder to overcome. A five or six-year-old is, generally, much easier and faster to teach than an adult. I can spend a summer trying to get an adult to TRULY relax and let the water hold them up.

WHY TEACH YOUR CHILD TO SWIM?

Drowning is scary. It's a silent killer. You don't hear a child slip under water; it's no movie scene of screaming and splashing. The quiet nature of drowning is why it happens to so many children even when under supervision[51].

The good news is that drowning is almost always preventable. Although no human is ever drown proof, no matter what the age, if your child is a confident and determined swimmer, they will be better equipped to navigate situations both in and out of the pool for the rest of their lives.

WHAT IS "DRY DROWNING"?

There is news media mayhem every summer talking about "dry drowning." It's scary, and there's a lot of social manipulation and distortion of facts. The benefit of the media frenzy is awareness. The downside is that it creates tension and, sometimes it even prevents parents from giving their children swimming lessons for fear of it happening.

It's important to note the terms "dry drowning," "delayed drowning," and "secondary drowning" are **not medical terms**. Medically, drowning can be fatal or non-fatal. It can be with injuries or without injuries. According to the World Health Organization, the medical definition of drowning is, "the process of experiencing respiratory impairment from submersion or immersion in liquid.[52]" Most groups, including the American Red Cross, The International Saving Life Federation, and World Health Organization, all discourage the use of terms "dry drowning," "delayed drowning," and "secondary drowning.[53]"

What are "Dry Drowning, Aspiration and Secondary drowning?"

"Dry Drowning" (Again, a non-medical term)

With "dry drowning" the water never reaches the lungs. "Dry Drowning" happens when someone breathes in water, and it causes his or her vocal cords to spasm and close up. You would notice your child having trouble breathing immediately if they were "dry drowning." The child would have trouble breathing, and the coloration of their face would change[54].

Aspiration: Aspiration is when something goes down your trachea (part of the respiratory system), instead of your esophagus (part of your digestive system). We have an epiglottis responsible for blocking food and water from getting into your airways, it works naturally. It flaps from one "tube" to the other, forcing the right substances down the correct pathways. If you get water "down the wrong tube" you, quite literally, get it down the wrong tube. Although rare, you can also aspirate part of a pretzel or even orange juice. Most of the time, if water or food goes down the wrong tube, you cough until your trachea is clear. If, in a rare occurrence, the substance gets into your lungs it can cause Pneumonia and other complications[55].

"Secondary drowning" (Also a non-medical term)

"Secondary drowning" is when the water gets into the lungs. It irritates the lining of the lungs and can cause respiratory failure. The media likes to make this type of fatal drowning seem like it's always fatal and that there are no signs or symptoms. This is not usually the case and as stated by the article, *"Secondary Drowning" in Children: An Important Message for All Parents* by Texas Children's Hospital, "Luckily, most healthy children who appear well after a submersion aspirate only small amount of water, if any, and will recover spontaneously.[56]"

When people ask me about "dry drowning," they are usually asking about "secondary drowning." The good news is, there are signs and symptoms In the article by WebMD "What is Dry-Drowning" says Mark Reiter, MD, past president of the American Academy of Emergency Medicine is quoted as saying,"The most likely course is that the symptoms are relatively mild and improve over time." The article continues on to say, "Any problems that do develop are usually treatable if you get medical care right away. Your job is to keep a close eye on your child for the 24 hours after he has had any problems in the water.[57]"

SIGNS AND SYMPTOMS:

If your child has recently been swimming and you notice[58]:

1) Persistent coughing
2) Difficulty breathing
3) Choking
4) Fatigue/ Lethargy or sleepiness
5) "Behavior shifts" – if your child is acting "off."/ Irritability
6) Vomiting
7) Loss of control of bowels
8) Blue/purple lips
9) Flaring of nostrils when breathing

If your child has any of these symptoms or any abnormal shift of behavior, call your pediatrician. If your child has an experience where they pass out underwater, or if they fall in or have a traumatic experience, it's always best to get them checked by a doctor.

How to Prevent Drowning?

The articles by Mayo Clinic[59], Healthline[60], USA Today[61], as well as the American Academy of Pediatrics, all have swimming lessons on their list of preventative measures against drowning.

CHAPTER 14:
Closing Thoughts

It's been a joy to be a part of your swim journey.

If you would like to help spread the word about swim safety, I'd love it if you would rate and review A MERMAID'S GUIDE on Amazon.   I read ALL the reviews, and am grateful for each and every one.

Thank you for joining me. Please feel free to reach out to me on Instagram at @Be_A_RBL. I'd love to share in your successes and assist you anyway I can.

Happy Swimming!

Hello friends? Still reading?

Want more tips, secrets, and insights delivered to your inbox?

Subscribe at www.relaxationbasedlifestyle.com to get

"The 27 Mermaid Secrets About Swimming, Revealed."

That's right. Two hundred and eighteen pages of swimming and I can keep going! The blogs debunk old, outdated swim methods in bite-size, humorous, and entertaining portions.

Five minutes to read, insights that last a lifetime.

XO

About the Author:

Michelle LANG

Michelle Lang, founder of RBL (pronounced "rebel"), for Relaxation Based Lifestyle, STUDIOS is a world class swim instructor, certified Reiki practitioner, black belt martial artist and filmmaker. A subsidiary of RBL, Michelle created the highly effective Relaxation Based Swimming Method to empower parents and their children with the proper tools to enjoy the water. Over the past 10 years, Michelle has established herself as the premiere swim instructor and travels around the globe to work with a wide variety of high-profile clients. A graduate of Northwestern University, Michelle currently lives in Los Angeles with her husband, filmmaker Ian Nelms, and their two little ones. For more information on Michelle and RBL, please visit www. RelaxationBasedLifestyle.com.

INSTAGRAM:

@Be_a_RBL for content to help you vacation your brain, daily.

@TheMichelleLang for travel and red carpet adventures.

@AMermaidsGuide for swim content!

Exercises and Techniques Co-created By:

Ian NELMS

Ian Nelms, an innovator of the Relaxation Based Swimming Method, is renowned for creating strong, confident swimmers. Drawing from his experience as a top national collegiate wrestler and MMA fighter, Ian uses his physical fitness to exemplify a warrior trait in and out of the water. Out of the pool, Ian is also an award-winning screenwriter, producer, and film director. Ian currently lives in Los Angeles with his wife, Michelle Lang, founder of RBL, and their two children. For more information on Ian, visit www.NelmsBros.com

Instagram/Twitter @TheNelmsBros

Glossary:

Pufferfish
What we do instead of blowing bubbles. Big breath, hold it and look like PUFFERFISH! Page 34

Moonwalk
No. Not Michael Jackson. This is when your child walks along the steps. It's a "moonwalk" because they take big steps like there's no gravity! Page 51

Chugga-Chugga
Also known as "Monkey Crawl" to some swim schools. The child uses their hands to move along the wall. Page 51

Hummmmm
How you feel about that sushi that you ate the other night...it wasn't bad...but it wasn't good. AND also what we do if a swimmer is having trouble modulating their breaths. Instead of blowing bubbles, have your child HUMMMM under the water. It lets the air out slower and helps your swimmer float longer! Page 53

Glides
Superman!!! (SuperWOMAN!!!) Straight arms and legs...gliding through the water to save the day. Page 66

Server Hold
Like you're presenting a massive tray of caviar. Use Server Hold to guide your swimmer back to the steps. Page 68

Child Control Hold (CCH)
Hold your child under their airmpits. Their hands can grip your arms. This hold gives your child the most secure feeling. Page 69

Teacher Control Hold (TCH)

Hold the child on the outside of their arms. In TCH your child CAN-NOT hold your arms. TCH allows you to control how much the water holds them. Page 69

Basketball Hold

Like you're shooting hoops with your kiddo! One hand goes under their bottom and the other under their armpit. Just like shooting a free throw, you'll use the backhand to push and the front hand to guide the shot. (And by "shot" I mean the gentle push to the steps.) Page 72

Floatie Magics

My FAVORITE! Your swimmer extends their arms and legs and allows the water to hold them up! No kicks, no arms. Just floating free. Page 74

Breath Expansion

Proper breath control is the most important part of learning to swim. Breath expansions give your child the skills they need to hold their breath long enough to get to safety or pop up for a breath. Page 77

Swimming with Intention

Being able to swim from point A to B without any external help. No undertow, no momentum. Being able to turn, get to the wall, or go back to the steps with ease. Page 79

Pizza Arms

What you have after your "carb cheat" day. AND a fun word for breaststroke arms. Teach breaststroke arms and flutter kicks to start. There's no point in learning freestyle arms until your child can pop up for breaths. Page 81

TAG

Having your swimmer "catch you." Page 82

Scoop Signs

The signs your child needs you to scoop them up. These are important so re-visit them! Page 74

Spin, Spin, Spin

Your child starts facing away from you and spins to you. This teaches them how to move and control their movements underwater. Page 89

U-Turn

Start your child on the step and have them turn and get back to you. Page 91

Swim Circle

The BEST way to get your child to relax and enjoy the water. Hard to describe in a few lines, so just go back to page 101!

Cobra

A way to practice popping up for breaths. The child leans backs and looks up the sky while you hold at various "pick points." Page 104

Deep Sea Diving

Diving to the bottom for toys. Page 107

Floatie Pops

The child does a Floatie Magic and then looks up the sky and says, "POP!" Page 188

My Turn, Your Turn

A good way to practice breaths: the child gets the first breath, you help them with the second breath. Page 110

Index

C

D

E

T

Endnotes

[1] National Vital Statistic System

[2] Ira Hyman Ph.D, Mind Reading Children, " Children can see your emotions and they learn to see your thoughts through your eyes. By age 4, most children can perform some mind reading" https://www.psychologytoday.com/us/blog/mental-mishaps/201007/mind-reading-children (July 16th, 2010)

[3] Cristi Vlad: The big 4 - Navy Seals Technique to conquering fear and panic. ttp://cristivlad.com/the-big-4-navy-seals-technique-conquering-fear-panic/ (Dec. 6, 2013)

[4] Tovah P. Klein, PhD "Toddlers want to be understood and validated in their desires." *How Toddlers Thrive* Touchstone (February 18, 2014)

[5] The International Center for Reiki Training, What is Reiki? *http://www.reiki.org/faq/whatisreiki.html*

[6]Benefits of Reiki for children *https://www.naturopathicme.com/benefits-reiki-children/*

[7] Morgan Rush (2017)The ideal temperature for swimming with babies. *https://www.livestrong.com/article/544037-the-ideal-temperature-for-swimming-with-babies/* (June 13, 2017)

[8]David DiSalvo (2013) Forbes / Pharma & Heahthcare Breathing and Your Brain, Five Reasons to Grab the Controls *https://www.forbes.com/sites/david-disalvo/2013/05/14/breathing-and-your-brain-five-reasons-to-grab-the-controls/#4365a1dc2d95*

[9] Lisa Firestone, PhD (2015) Psychology Today 5

Ways to Build Trust and Honesty in your Relationship https://www.psychologytoday.com/us/blog/compassion-matters/201506/5-ways-build-trust-and-honesty-in-your-relationship

[10] Apryl Duncan (2018) Very Well Family; Why playing alone is important for children. https://www.verywellfamily.com/why-playing-alone-is-important-3129415 (April 5th, 2018)

[11] Tovah P. Klein, PhD "Toddlers are all about trying, regardless of the outcome." *How Toddlers Thrive* Touchstone (February 18, 2014)

[12] MGB Mindfulness; The Seven Chakras for beginners. https://www.mindbodygreen.com/0-91/The-7-Chakras-for-Beginners.html (Oct. 28, 2009)

[13] PsycoloGenie *https://psycologcnie.com/psychology-behind-golem-effect* (March 2, 2018)

[14] Vanessa Van Edwards; Captivate *"As humans we are constantly on the look out for people who are similar to us."* Portfolio (April 25, 2017)

[15] Vanessa Van Edwards; Captivate "Why is eye contact so powerful? It produces oxytocin, the chemical foundation for trust." Portfolio (April 25, 2017)

[16] Child Mind Institute: How to Give Kids Effective Instructions https://childmind.org/article/how-to-give-kids-effective-instructions/

[17] Karen Spangenberg Postal Ph.D., A.B.P.P. How Structure Approves Your Child's Brain https://www.psychologytoday.com/us/blog/think-better/201111/how-structure-improves-your-childs-brain (Nov. 11, 2011)

[18] Vanessa LoBue, Assistant Professor of Psychology, Rutgers University Newark Face time: here's how infants learn from facial expressions: "Around

eight to 12 months of age, infants learn that they can use information from other people's faces – especially their mom's – to help them figure out what to do in new situations."http://theconversation.com/face-time-heres-how-infants-learn-from-facial-expressions-53327 (Jan. 26, 2016)

[19] Kids Health; Water Safety https://kidshealth. org/en/parents/water-safety.html (June 2014)

[20] Your Child's Growing Brain: Ages 5-8 https:// www.babycenter.com/0_your-childs-growing-brain-ages-5-to-8_3659070.bc

[21] Bably Milestone: Walking https://www.baby-center.com/0_baby-milestone-walking_6507.bc

[22] Deborah Kotz (2008) Time In the Sun: How Much Is Needed for Vitamin D? https://health.usnews.com/ health-news/family-health/heart/articles/2008/06/23/ time-in-the-sun-how-much-is-needed-for-vitamin-d (June 23, 2008)

[23] Danielle Dellorto CNN https://www.cnn. com/2012/05/16/health/sunscreen-report/index.html (May 16, 2012)

[24] Rebecca Adams HuffPost Wellness: What happens when food goes 'down the wrong pipe."*https:// www.huffingtonpost.com/2014/03/06/food-down-the-wrong-pipe_n_4889910.html (March 6, 2013)*

[25] SEEKER, Video What Holding your Breath Does to your Body *https://www.youtube.com/ watch?v=phpbZqlPHXk*

[26] Dopamine Lollipops: Dr. John Medina's Brain Rules *http://nasje.org/dopamine-lollipops-dr-john-medinas-brain-rules/ (December 22nd, 2015)*

[27] Craig Freudenrich, PhD How Stuff Works; How

your Lungs Work *https://health.howstuffworks.com/human-body/systems/respiratory/lung3.htm*

[28] TIME HEALTH; 7 workout habits you should drop now *http://time.com/9278/7-workout-habits-you-should-drop-now/ (Feb. 22, 2014)*

[29] Parmjit Singh, PhD Breathing and Mental States *http://www.parmjitsingh.com/?p=554*

[30] Melodie Anne LIVESTRONG Burping while Swimming *https://www.livestrong.com/article/551401-burping-while-swimming/*

[31] American Red Cross: Reach or Throw, Don't Go *http://www.redcross.org/images/MEDIA_CustomProductCatalog/m44240110_Reach_or_throw_dont_go.pdf*

[32] KKCO News 11 *"Pool Manager Pete Ashman says most common floatation devices give parents a false sense of security when it comes to pool safety, "The water wings the rings the noodles all float but they don't necessarily hold people up the way that they need to be held up in order to keep from going under water and potentially drowning." http://www.nbc11news.com/home/headlines/98639404.html*

[33] David A. Carbonell, PhD The Worry Trick *"Why doesn't the cerebral cortex tell the amygdala to stand down? Because the nervous connections between the amygdala and cerebral cortex only allow for one way communication." New Harbinger Publications; 1 edition (February 2, 2016)*

[34] Suzanne Schlosberg PARENTING Separation Anxiety Age-by-Age *https://www.parenting.com/article/separation-anxiety-age-by-age*

[35] David A. Carbonell, PhD The Worry Trick *New Harbinger Publications; 1 edition (February 2, 2016)*

[36] Center on the Developing Child Harvard University Executive Function and Self-Regulation *https://developingchild.harvard.edu/science/key-concepts/executive-function/*

[37] Child Mind Institute: How Can we Help Kids with Self-Regulation? *https://childmind.org/article/can-help-kids-self-regulation/*

[38] Roberta Michnick Golinkoff and Kathy Hirsh-Pasek Co-written with Vinaya Rajan, Ph.D, HUFF-POST Self-Regulation: Just as Important as Learning Your ABCs and 123 *https://www.huffingtonpost.com/roberta-michnick-golinkoff/selfregulation-just-as-im_b_5675896.html*

[39] Tovah P. Klein, PhD *How Toddlers Thrive* Touchstone (February 18, 2014)

[40] Harvey Karp, M.D. Happiest Toddler on The Block "Try not to make wobbly limits!" Bantam Dell Publishing (September, 2008)

[41] Sherrie Campbell, PhD HuffPost: 7Ways to Unlock Your Greatness *https://www.huffingtonpost.com/sherrie-campbell-phd/7-ways-to-unlock-your-greatness_b_9206552.html (Feb 14, 2014)*

[42] Olivia Chapman, COASTSPORT PHYSIO and SPORTS MEDICINE, Respiratory Dysfunction in Swimmers http://coastsport.com.au/resp_swim/ (Feb. 6, 2016)

[43] Alexandra Momyer LIVESTRONG Sore Stomach After I Swim https://www.livestrong.com/article/439311-sore-stomach-after-i-swim/ (SEPT. 11, 2017)

[44] Andrew Newberg, M.D. and Mark Waldman PSYCHOLOGY TODAY The Most Dangerous Word in

the World https://www.psychologytoday.com/us/blog/words-can-change-your-brain/201207/the-most-dangerous-word-in-the-world (Aug 01, 2012)

[44] Donna B. Pincus, Ph.D. HUFFPOST Helping Kids Get Past the Fear of Trying Something New https://www.huffingtonpost.com/donna-b-pincus-phd/kids-fear_b_1725248.html (August 01, 2012)

[45] Loris Malaguzzi, founder of the Reggio-Emilia method THE REGGIO EMILIA APPROACH http://www.chevychasereggio.com/reggio%20emilia%20approach.htm

[46] Saul McLeod Id, Ego and Superego https://www.simplypsychology.org/psyche.html (2016)

[47] Ethos3 The Importance of Non-Verbal Communication https://www.ethos3.com/speaking-tips/the-importance-of-non-verbal-communication/

[48] Know the Functions of Epiglottis and the Problem: Epiglottitis http://www.newhealthguide.org/Epiglottis-Function.html

[49] Baby milestone: Walking https://www.babycenter.com/0_baby-milestone-walking_6507.bc

[50] AAP Gives Updated Advice on Drowning Prevention https://www.aap.org/en-us/about-the-aap/aap-press-room/pages/AAP-Gives-Updated-Advice-on-Drowning-Prevention.aspx (May 24, 2010)

[51] News Medical Life Sciences 88 percent of children who drown are under the supervision of another person https://www.news-medical.net/news/2004/04/28/998.aspx (April 28, 2004)

[52] E.F. van Beeck, C.M. Branche, D. Szpilman, J.H. Modell, & J.J.L.M. Bierens A new definition of drowning: towards documentation and prevention of a

global public health problem *http://www.who.int/bulle-tin/volumes/83/11/vanbeeck1105abstract/en/*

[53] *Drowning in a Sea of Misinformation: Dry Drowning and Secondary Drowning https://journals. lww.com/em-news/blog/BreakingNews/pages/post. aspx?PostID=377 (June 16, 2017)*

[54] *Reviewed By Robert Mcnamara, MD, faaem Laryngospasm (Dry Drowning) Near Drowning Drown-ing https://www.philacanoe.org/resources/Documents/ cold%20water%20safety/Laryngospasm-secondary%20 drowning-near%20drowning.pdf*

[55] *HealthLine What happens when you aspirate? https://www.healthline.com/health/aspiration*

[56] *Texas Children's Hospital "Secondary Drown-ing" in Children: An Important Message for All Parents https://www.texaschildrens.org/blog/2014/06/second-ary-drowning%E2%80%9D-children-important-mes-sage-all-parents (June 6, 2014)*

[57] *Amanda Gardner Reviewed by Neha Pathak, MD WEB MD What Is 'Dry Drowning'? https://www. webmd.com/children/features/secondary-drowning-dry-drowning#2 (June 29, 2017)*

[58] *Salil Pradhan, MD, Ask a Doc: What's the difference between dry drowning and secondary drowning? https://www.usatoday.com/story/life/all-themoms/2018/06/01/dry-drowning-secondary-drown-ing-difference/663359002/ (June 1, 2018)*

[59] *Water safety: Protect your child from drown-ing https://www.mayoclinic.org/healthy-lifestyle/infant-and-toddler-health/in-depth/child-safety/art-20044744*

[60] *Kathryn Watson, Medically reviewed by Karen Gill, MD What Is Dry Drowning? https://www.health-*

line.com/health/dry-drowning#prevention (June 1, 2018)

[61] Salil Pradhan, MD, Ask a Doc: What's the difference between dry drowning and secondary drowning?https://www.usatoday.com/story/life/allthe-moms/2018/06/01/dry-drowning-secondary-drowning-difference/663359002/

45070548R00146

Made in the USA
Middletown, DE
13 May 2019